Living in Imperial China

EXPLORING
CULTURAL
HISTORY

Jann Einfeld, *Book Editor*

Bruce Glassman, *Vice President*
Bonnie Szumski, *Publisher*
Helen Cothran, *Managing Editor*

**GREENHAVEN
PRESS®**

THOMSON
™
GALE

San Diego • Detroit • New York • San Francisco • Cleveland
New Haven, Conn. • Waterville, Maine • London • Munich

THOMSON

GALE

LIBRARY OF CONGRESS CATALOGING-IN-PUBLICATION DATA

Living in imperial China / Jann Einfeld, book editor.
    p. cm. — (Exploring cultural history)
Includes bibliographical references and index.
ISBN 0-7377-2090-5 (lib. bdg. : alk. paper)
    1. China—Social life and customs. I. Einfeld, Jann. II. Series.
DS721.L67776 2004
951—dc22   2003068591

Printed in the United States of America

Contents

Chapter 1: Families and Domestic Life

yin and yang underlay all of nature, and illness was caused by an imbalance in these forces.

Chapter 2: Religions and Rituals

Chapter 3: Working Life

Chapter 4: The Arts and Entertainment

Foreword

Too often, history books and teachers place an overemphasis on events and dates. Students learn that key births, battles, revolutions, coronations, and assassinations occurred in certain years. But when many centuries separate these happenings from the modern world, they can seem distant, disconnected, even irrelevant.

The reality is that today's society is *not* disconnected from the societies that preceded it. In fact, modern culture is a sort of melting pot of various aspects of life in past cultures. Over the course of centuries and millennia, one culture passed on some of its traditions, in the form of customs, habits, ideas, and beliefs, to another, which modified and built on them to fit its own needs. That culture then passed on its own version of the traditions to later cultures, including today's. Pieces of everyday life in past cultures survive in our own lives, therefore. And it is often these morsels of tradition, these survivals of tried and true past experience, that people most cherish, take comfort in, and look to for guidance. As the great English scholar and archaeologist Sir Leonard Woolley put it, "We cannot divorce ourselves from our past. We are always conscious of precedents . . . and we let experience shape our views and actions."

Thus, for example, Americans and the inhabitants of a number of other modern nations can pride themselves on living by the rule of law, educating their children in formal schools, expressing themselves in literature and art, and following the moral precepts of various religions and philosophies. Yet modern society did not invent the laws, schools, literature, art, religions, and philosophies that pervade it; rather, it inherited these things from previous cultures. "Time, the great destroyer, is also the great preserver," the late, noted thinker Herbert J. Muller once observed. "It has preserved . . . the immense accumulation of products, skills, styles, customs, institutions, and ideas that make the man on the American street indebted to all the peoples of history, including some who never saw a street." In this way, ancient Mesopotamia gave the world its first cities and literature; ancient Egypt, large-scale architecture; ancient Israel, the formative concepts of Judaism,

6

Christianity, and Islam; ancient Greece, democracy, the theater, Olympic sports, and magnificent ceramics; ancient China, gunpowder and exotic fabrics; ancient Rome and medieval England, their pioneering legal systems; Renaissance Italy, great painting and sculpture; Elizabethan England, the birth of modern drama; and colonial America, the formative environments of the founders of the United States, the most powerful and prosperous nation in world history. Only by looking back on those peoples and how they lived can modern society understand its roots.

Not all the products of cultural history have been so constructive, however. Most ancient Greeks severely restricted the civil rights and daily lives of women, for instance; the Romans kept and abused large numbers of slaves, as did many Americans in the years preceding the Civil War; and Nazi Germany and the Soviet Union curbed or suppressed freedom of speech, assembly, and religion. Examining these negative aspects of life in various past cultures helps to expose the origins of many of the social problems that exist today; it also reminds us of the ever-present potential for people to make mistakes and pursue misguided or destructive social and economic policies.

The books in the Greenhaven Press Exploring Cultural History series provide readers with the major highlights of life in human cultures from ancient times to the present. The family, home life, food and drink, women's duties and rights, childhood and education, arts and leisure, literacy and literature, roads and means of communications, slavery, religious beliefs, and more are examined in essays grouped by theme. The essays in each volume have been chosen for their readability and edited to manageable lengths. Many are primary sources. These original voices from a past culture echo through the corridors of time and give the volume a strong feeling of immediacy and authenticity. The other essays are by historians and other modern scholars who specialize in the culture in question. An annotated table of contents, chronology, and extensive bibliography broken down by theme add clarity and context. Thus, each volume in the Greenhaven Press Exploring Cultural History series opens a unique window through which readers can gaze into a distant time and place and eavesdrop on life in a long vanished culture.

Introduction

A way of life is subtly and inextricably bound up with the ideas
that belong to it, and no doubt this provides the real explanation
for our interest in the details of daily life when we study the history of a people.

—Jacques Gernet, cultural historian[1]

A succession of seventy-six emperors ruled the vast land of
China from 206 B.C. until A.D. 1911, qualifying China's imperial age as the longest-surviving political era in history. Its longevity is all the more significant, as China, then as now, was the
most populous country on earth. "None of the great European
dynasties—the [Austrian] Hapsburgs (1273–1919), the [Russian]
Romanovs (1613–1917), or the Norman and Plantagenet kings
of England (1066–1485)—ruled as large a state as China, with
such a monopoly of power . . . [and] neither Japan, India, nor
Persia produced regimes comparable in scope and power,"[2] writes
historian John King Fairbank.

The longevity and scope of the imperial order were not the
only remarkable features of China's era of empires. Throughout
the six major dynasties—the Han (206 B.C.–A.D. 220), the Tang
(619–906), the Song (960–1279), the Yuan (1279–1368), the
Ming (1368–1644), and the Qing (1644–1912)—China experienced extraordinary cultural continuity. For more than two
thousand years, the home and work life, religious rituals, and
leisure activities of the imperial Chinese remained remarkably
consistent. "Despite some innovations that had come about,"
notes cultural historian Michael Loewe, "[by the late imperial
era] there were still many aspects of Chinese life which had been
formed in the earliest days of imperial history and which bore
unmistakable marks of the societies of those remote days."[3]

A crucial aspect of the cultural continuity of imperial China
was the belief systems on which the society was based. From the
early days of the Han emperors, the imperial Chinese were divided by sharp disparities of wealth, education, and social status,
but united by a common vision of the virtuous society. The
source of virtue that linked the peasant with the emperor, the
living with the dead, and the human with the natural worlds was

filial piety, or duty of children to parents. Honoring filial obligations was the organizing principle of imperial Chinese society and the central value that guided people's daily lives.

Yin and Yang Theory of the Universe

Ancient Chinese society had a distinctive view of creation and the forces that control the natural world. The ancient Chinese believed the universe came into being from the spontaneous interaction of two primal forces—yang and yin. Yang was the force associated with action, heat, light, and masculinity, while yin was the force associated with compliance, cold, darkness, and femininity. Through the first interaction of yang and yin the five primary elements were created—fire (from yang), water (from yin), and earth, wood, and metal (from combinations of yin and yang). These elements combined to create heaven, which was mostly yang, and earth, which was more yin. The ancient Chinese classic *The Book of Changes* states: "The *yin* and *yang* unite their forces, and the hard and the soft gain embodiment, thus giving manifestation to the phenomena of Heaven and Earth."[4]

Heaven and earth were not the only manifestations of yin and yang. The Chinese believed that every element of the universe—the sun and the moon, the emperor and his subjects, men and women—were all associated with yin or yang. Although yin and yang forces were equally essential to the health of the universe, they were not equal. Their creative powers were unleashed when their opposite and complementary energies were ordered in a hierarchy in which yang was above yin. Every facet of life in the human and natural worlds was bound in these yin-yang hierarchies—heaven (yang) was above earth (yin); men (yang) were above women (yin); and parents (yang) were the dominant force in relation to children (yin). Even the human body consisted of complementary, hierarchically organized parts associated with yin and yang. For example, the heart was considered yang while the lungs were seen as subservient yin.

When yin and yang energies were in perfect balance, the Chinese believed that a divine energy called qi was free to circulate throughout the macrocosmic and microcosmic worlds to create health, harmony, and prosperity. Conversely, blockage of the flow of chi was the root cause of all disease and disorder. The third-century B.C. scholar Lushi chunqui explained the consequences of stagnant qi:

> When [a person's] illness lasts and pathology develops, it is because the essential *ch'i* has become static. Analogously, stagnant water becomes foul, a tree when [the circulation of qi] is stagnant becomes worm-eaten; grasses [when the circulation of their qi is] stagnant becomes withered. . . . States too have their stases. When the ruler's virtue does not flow freely [i.e., when he is out of touch with his subjects], and the wishes of his people do not reach him, this is the stasis of a state. When the stasis of a state abides for a long time . . . the cruelty of those above and those below each other arises from this.[5]

Interdependence Between Humanity and the Cosmos

Not only did the imperial Chinese believe that qi flowed through the heart of all the living systems in the cosmos, but they also viewed all these systems as connected to one another—the universe, nature, and humanity were linked so that the fate of one was tied to the fate of the other. Natural catastrophes like earthquakes or floods had dire consequences for human beings, and human misconduct could adversely impact the natural order. Second-century Chinese scholar Ch'un-ch'iu fan lu explained the relationship between human conduct and the flow of qi:

> As a result of human order or disorder, dynamic or quiescent *ch'i*, compliant or contrary *ch'i* will detract from or add to the transforming power of *yin* and *yang*, affecting all within the four seas. . . . When the world is well ordered and the people are at peace, when the will of the ruler is settled and the *ch'i* [that energizes the political order] is rectified, the transforming power of heaven and earth operates in a state of perfection and among the myriad things only the finest are produced. But when the world is in disorder and the people are perverse, when the will of the ruler is depraved and the [ordering] *ch'i* is contrary, the transforming power of Heaven and Earth is impaired and calamities arise.[6]

Human beings were connected to the natural realm through their relationship with a supreme deity called Tian, or Heaven. While Heaven had the power to create or destroy life, it did not transcend nature, but was a working part of it. Heaven bestowed its mandate on the Chinese emperor as the "son of Heaven" and vested him with the power to preserve or destroy life.

Confucian Filial Piety

To ensure the continuation of life in the cosmos, the emperor was expected to conduct rites and rituals in accordance with the doctrine of Confucianism, the dominant spiritual tradition of imperial China. Established by the early Han emperors as the ideology of the state, Confucianism was a code of ethics, rather than a formal religion, and was based on the teaching of the sixth-century B.C. sage, Confucius (551–479 B.C.).

Confucius believed that people's first obligation was to live in proper relations with those around them: "If I am not a man among men, then what am I?" Confucius said. Confucius defined individuals through their observance of reciprocal obligations that connected them to every other member of imperial society. These obligations were governed by the principle of filial piety that required that people always act in ways that would honor the sacred inheritance bestowed on them by their ancestors. Children were obliged to obey their parents, and in turn, parents were required to act in ways appropriate to their position of authority. One family advice manual from the sixteenth-century Ming dynasty stated:

> Parents have special responsibilities. *The Book of Changes* says: "The members of a family have strict sovereigns." These sovereigns are the parents. Their position in a family is one of unique authority, and they should utilize their authority to dictate matters, to maintain order, and to inspire respect, so that the members of the family will be obedient. . . . The elders must demand discipline of themselves, following all rules and regulations to the letter, so that the younger members emulate their good behavior.[7]

Confucius believed that filial piety was the moral sanction for all human action. He drew his inspiration from the twelfth-century B.C. Zhou kings, who had used this principle to establish peace and prosperity among the ancient Chinese. "Filial piety was the surpassing virtue and essential way the early kings kept the world in order, the people in harmony both with their relatives and at large, and all, both high and low, uncomplaining,"[8] Confucius said.

Filial Piety Orders Imperial Society

Confucianism established filial piety as the governing principle of imperial society. Designed to promote the virtues of loyalty, reverence, consideration of others, and diligence in serving one's superiors, it connected all social classes in mutual obligations based on codes of conduct elaborated by Confucian scholars. At the apex of the social hierarchy was the emperor. As the son of Heaven and the patriarch of the people, the emperor was expected to honor his ancestral obligations and tend to the welfare of his subjects. The emperor's filial obligations included conducting elaborate rituals in honor of Heaven as well as seven generations of his earthly ancestors, and educating the people in their filial duties. *The Classic of Filiality* states, "One who is a worthy ruler . . . dutifully serves his ancestors, establishes academies . . . in towns and villages to teach filial piety . . ., enlightens [the people] with education, moves [them] with rites and music . . . and serves the foundation of Heaven in this way."[9]

To serve Heaven the emperor required the advice of learned scholars to interpret the complex requirements of the classical Confucian texts. Scholars became officials in the government bureaucracy and were expected to perpetuate Confucian values by encouraging the people to honor their filial obligations. The principle filial obligation of scholar-officials was to be loyal to the emperor. As *The Classic of Filiality* states, "If one serves one's prince with the filiality one shows one's father, it becomes the virtue of fidelity (loyalty). . . . Thus one may preserve one's rank and office. . . . This is the filiality of the scholar official."[10]

Farmers were accorded the next highest status in the Confucian hierarchy after scholar-officials. Farmers, who were the largest vocational group, were respected because they provided food for the people and revenue for the imperial coffers. Confucian codes of conduct for fulfilling the farmers' filial obligations emphasized living in harmony with nature and diligently carrying out their daily activities. "In keeping with Heaven's seasons and Earth's resources, by one's industry and frugality one supports one's father and mother. This is the filiality of the common people,"[11] said the classical texts. At the base of the Confucian imperial hierarchy were the merchants and businessmen. In order to fulfill their societal filial obligations, Confucius instructed merchants to keep profits low and to be lenient when peasants could not pay their debts.

Filial Piety and the Supernatural World

The principle of filial piety also governed the relations between the people and the supernatural world. From the beginning of their civilization, the Chinese believed that the souls of their departed family members could affect the family destiny. Deceased ancestors continued to play an important role in family life and were called on to guide the patriarch in important decisions, bless a new wife or baby, or witness the scolding of an errant child.

Filial obligations of the imperial Chinese continued after the death of the parents. Confucian traditions stipulated precise rituals for honoring ancestral spirits. When a parent died, drops of his or her blood were placed on ancestral tablets in order to capture his or her spirit. Tablets were placed on ancestral altars featured in every Chinese household, and regular sacrifices of food and wine were laid out to feed the "hungry ghosts" of dead parents and grandparents. Sacrifices were generally made every two weeks in ceremonies in which the eldest son would act as the spirit medium for his ancestors and communicate messages from the family's relatives in the astral realm.

Worship of the dead was not confined to people's family members. Deceased dignitaries were honored during many Chinese festivals throughout the year. Confucius believed that revering authority figures of the past through the practice of rituals was the key to promoting harmony among the living and between the living and the dead. He said, "[Through the practice of rituals] the living were at peace; and in death, content. Thus with all under Heaven at peace, no calamities [could] occur, no disasters [arise]."[12]

The Significance of Filial Piety

Although the vast mass of the Chinese peasantry lived in small rural villages and had no direct contact with the emperor, every Chinese child learned to honor his or her parents and revere the family ancestors. Socialization in the nuclear family became the training ground for developing loyalty to the emperor and diligence in serving those superior in the imperial hierarchy. Filial piety was the means through which the Chinese emperors succeeded in governing the largest number of people with the least direct intervention of any known political system. "One need not be obsessed with the merits of the Chinese," said the philosopher Voltaire in 1785, "to recognize that the organization of their empire is in truth the best that the world has ever seen."[13]

The organization of imperial Chinese society was based on a unique worldview that equated political order with moral and cosmic order. Fulfilling filial obligations promoted order in the family, in the society, and in the cosmos, inviting the free flow of heavenly qi to bring health and harmony to all the interconnected systems of the universe. Almost a century after the end of the imperial era, family loyalty, reverence for elders, worship of ancestral spirits, and harmony with nature remain an integral part of contemporary Chinese cultural life. Filial piety, as a compelling moral value, served as the ordering principle of the most enduring political framework yet invented by humankind.

*   *   *   *   *

A Note on Chinese Pinyin Language

Chinese written language is readable to Chinese people everywhere regardless of the dialect spoken. However, Chinese language makes little sense to Westerners unless they are trained to read the characters. Systems of transliterating these characters—that is, changing them into a different alphabet—have been developed to make it possible for Westerners to read Chinese.

There are two systems of transliteration. The Wade-Giles system was used for many years, and this system is still found in many older books. The pinyin system was officially adopted by the Chinese government during the 1950s and is used everywhere today in China. When pinyin was established, names such as *Peking* under the Wade-Giles system became *Beijing. Mao Tsetung* became *Mao Zedong*.

This book generally uses the pinyin system. However, if an article was written using the Wade-Giles system, that system is retained.

Regarding Chinese names: The surname (family name) is given first and the personal name follows. For example, *Mao* is Mao Zedong's surname.

Notes

1. Jacques Gernet, *Daily Life in China on the Eve of the Mongol Invasion, 1250–1276.* Stanford, CA: Stanford University Press, 1962, p. 197.

2. John King Fairbank, *China: A New History.* Cambridge, MA: Harvard University Press, 1992, p. 46.

3. Michael Loewe, *Everyday Life in Early Imperial China During the Han Period, 202 B.C.–A.D. 220.* New York: Dorset Press, 1968, p. 28.

4. Quoted in Derk Bodde, *Essays on Chinese Civilization.* Princeton, NJ: Princeton University Press, 1981, p. 280.

5. Quoted in Nathan Sivin, "State, Cosmos, and Body in the Last Three Centuries B.C.," *Harvard Journal of Asiatic Studies,* June 1995, p. 20.

6. Sivin, "State, Cosmos, and Body in the Last Three Centuries B.C.," p. 27.

7. Quoted in Patricia Buckley Ebrey, ed., *Chinese Civilization and Society: A Sourcebook.* New York: Free Press, 1981, p. 278.

8. Quoted in William Theodore de Bary and Irene Bloom, eds., *Sources of Chinese Tradition,* vol. 1. New York: Columbia University Press, 1999, p. 326.

9. Quoted in de Bary and Bloom, *Sources of Chinese Tradition,* p. 300.

10. Quoted in de Bary and Bloom, *Sources of Chinese Tradition,* p. 327.

11. Quoted in de Bary and Bloom, *Sources of Chinese Tradition,* p. 327.

12. Quoted in de Bary and Bloom, *Sources of Chinese Tradition,* p. 328.

13. Quoted in Bodde, *Essays on Chinese Civilization,* p. 137.

Families and Domestic Life

CHAPTER
1

Chapter Preface

In imperial China the principle of hierarchy organized society and daily life, including family relationships, the roles of males and females, and even the design of Chinese houses and fashion. In the family hierarchy, the father was the supreme autocrat. Under imperial law, he could sell his children into slavery or execute them for improper conduct, though this rarely occurred. Even though age was accorded higher status than youth in the family hierarchy, males dominated females of any age. Therefore, the eldest son had rights and privileges not accorded to his mother. The extended family was also a complex hierarchy of uncles, aunts, in-laws, cousins, and other members who had obligations to each other, including calling particular family members by the appropriate title befitting their status in the family hierarchy.

Within the nuclear family, males and females were segregated at an early age. At seven, boys and girls no longer ate together or sat on the same mat. At ten, boys from more privileged families left home to be tutored in reading, writing, and the skills of archery and chariot driving. At around the age of twenty, they studied ceremonial procedures to prepare them for married life, which usually began in their thirties. Girls, on the other hand, stayed at home to study with a governess who taught them basic etiquette, sewing, weaving, and the preparation of food for rituals and ceremonies. They pinned up their hair at sixteen to signal their eligibility for courtship. When a girl married, usually at around twenty, she moved to her husband's household, where she was expected to defer to her mother-in-law.

In their husband's household, women continued to lead lives separate from the men. One family manual that prescribed rules for the conduct of family members advised that "Men and women should not sit together or use the same hangers, towels, or combs." The design of the typical Chinese home reinforced this separation of the sexes. Outer buildings were occupied by male family members, and inner chambers by female family members. The outer and inner areas were separated by a courtyard to further ensure that men and women had little physical contact.

Women's activities in the inner chambers of the house were

more restricted than men's. Furthermore, women's fashions reinforced their circumscribed lives and dependence on the male
household members. The popular practice of foot binding, which
began in the tenth century among upper-class women, was one
way in which fashion limited women's lives. Girls began the foot
binding preparations when they were about six years old. Their
arches were bent, their toes curled under, and their feet were
bound in tight bandages. Their crippled feet ensured that females
could not venture far from home without being carried or accompanied by male household members. This served to reinforce
their dependent and lesser status within the family. Husbands
and fathers took great pride in boasting of the small size of their
wives' or daughters' feet.

Just as the family hierarchy determined the status of its members, the hierarchy of society in imperial China determined the
status of its members and even the kind of clothing the people
in each class wore. The lower classes wore black and white, or
light-colored long, plain shirts with pants or skirts. The upper
classes, on the other hand, wore brilliant purple, scarlet, aqua,
or green full-length robes with embroidered golden dragons and
phoenixes. Within the upper classes of society, dress codes were
elaborated to reflect further distinctions of status. For example,
until the tenth century, only the princes of the imperial family
were allowed to carry turquoise silk parasols. Similarly, officials
were allowed to wear only colors that designated their status in
the imperial bureaucracy.

The Chinese believed that failing to adhere to the duties and
conventions of their roles within the family and the social hierarchy would harm the health and weaken the longevity of the
group. They valued the qualities of obedience and deference to
authority. "The filial piety [obligations to parents] and obedience
inculcated in family life," writes historian John King Fairbank in
China: A New History, "were the training ground for loyalty to the
ruler and obedience to the constituted authority in the state."
Despite over a century of exposure to Western influences, the
Chinese family today retains many such traditional values.

Patriarchal Families of Imperial China

Martin K. Whyte

According to the Confucian tradition of imperial China, the ideal society rested on a vast hierarchy of mutual obligations among all its members, from the lowliest peasant to the emperor. At the base of this structure was the patriarchal Chinese family. In the following extract, Martin K. Whyte says that Chinese families were organized in a hierarchy in which the younger members deferred to the older members, and the female members deferred to the male members. The patriarch made the major family decisions, and all his family members were expected to respect his authority. In the same way, all the subjects of the realm were expected to obey the rule of the emperor. Whyte states that while the imperial order and the traditional Chinese family provided security and stability for the people, their freedom to make choices about their lives and to express their own ideas was limited. Martin K. Whyte is a professor of Chinese studies at the Center for Chinese Studies at the University of Michigan. In his most recent publication, *China's Revolutions and Intergenerational Relations*, which he edited in 2003, he says that many characteristics of the traditional Chinese family are still evident in contemporary Chinese culture.

Chinese society in late imperial times was shaped by a set of Confucian assumptions and values about the ideal society. In this Confucian framework, the cement that held society together was supposed to be moral consensus, and the building blocks that were held together by this cement were human bonds and mutual obligations arranged in a vast hierarchy—from emperor and ministers down through local officials and local gentry, and finally to the immediate family—the bonds between father and son, husband and wife, brother and brother, and so

Martin K. Whyte, *The Chinese: Adapting the Past, Building the Future*, edited by Robert F. Dernberger. Ann Arbor: The University of Michigan Center for Chinese Studies, 1986. Copyright © 1986 by The University of Michigan Center for Chinese Studies.

on. It was assumed that a uniform, "correct" set of values and rules of behavior could be specified for all of the links in this complex human chain of relationships; in the ideal society, systematic instruction in these proper rules, and group pressure to comply with them, would produce social harmony and prosperity. This sort of emphasis led to a very different view of politics and the role of the state from that which developed in the pluralist, competitive West, a view in which officials were as much preachers as administrators.

These themes in the Chinese tradition did, in fact, lead to a variety of interesting attempts at moral indoctrination that anticipate the study of [revolutionary leader] Mao Zedong's thought in contemporary China. For example, during the Qing Dynasty [1644–1911] local officials were required to have lectures on Confucian moral homilies given regularly in market towns throughout the realm, and righteous individuals and virtuous widows were publicly honored, sometimes with memorial arches to commemorate them. Still, officials and political philosophers did not think that social order could be maintained simply by preaching to the population. Most people were not educated or enlightened enough to understand and obey the dictates of Confucian principles, but they could be expected to conform to the demands of their parents, their teachers, and their employers or patrons. Thus, ideally Chinese society should have no autonomous individuals or deviant subcultures. Instead, all individuals should be members of one or more groups or social networks which would lock them into a chain of obligations that linked them ultimately to the state. Political order would rest not upon a sense of citizenship, but upon this hierarchical chain of personal ties and mutual obligations.

In many ways the Chinese family was viewed as the key to a good society, since for most of the population family interactions and obligations far outweighed any other social bonds. Many traditional writings on social order in China used family images for the entire imperial hierarchy, from the emperor as the "son of heaven" through the "father-mother officials" (*fumu guan*) down to the actual families in local communities. In a very loose sense, then, the entire society was seen as one vast, extended family ruled over by a paternalistic emperor, and only if family bonds and socialization were developed properly throughout China could social harmony reign. A passage from the *Great Learning*, one of the "Four Books" that formed the core of Confucian learning, conveys this set of assumptions:

> By enquiring into all things, understanding is made complete; with complete understanding, thought is made sincere; when thought is sincere, the mind is as it should be; when the mind is as it should be, the individual is morally cultivated; when the individual is morally cultivated, the family is well regulated; when the family is well regulated, the state is properly governed; and when the state is properly governed the world is at peace.

Rigid Hierarchy

The form of family life that had evolved in China by late imperial times conformed to this imagery of strict, hierarchical role relationships and was thus in many respects different from family forms in the contemporary West. Individuals were born into not only a family but a patrilineal kin group, and in some parts of China entire rural villages of several thousand people belonged to a single lineage (sometimes called a Chinese "clan"). Both patrilineages and the families that comprised them were organized hierarchically, with younger members and females expected to show deference and respect for elder members and males. From infancy onward Chinese were instructed in obedience to the family and "filial piety," an ethic of worshipful deference toward one's parents. (This extreme emphasis on respect toward one's elders extended even beyond the grave in the form of ancestor worship rituals at graves and in lineage halls.) All members of the family were expected to defer to the will of the family patriarch who, as the representative of the patrilineal line and the head of the corporate family, was supposed to make binding decisions that would promote the interests of the family as a whole. Although most Chinese spent much of their lives in nuclear family units, rather than in the multi-generational, extended families that form most Westerners' image of China, still a small family could be a fairly authoritarian place in comparison with Western families as we know them today.

Perhaps nothing better illustrates the strong emphases on group loyalty and the internal hierarchy of the Chinese family than the dominant set of marriage customs in late imperial times. Marriages were customarily arranged by parents with the aid of hired marriage go-betweens. In many if not most cases the result might be termed "blind marriage"—the bride and groom did not even meet until the day of the wedding. Since the maturity, compatibility, or consent of the couple were not required, marriages were sometimes arranged between children or between a boy and a mature woman, or vice versa. And since divorce was strongly discouraged, the couple, never having met and often poorly matched, were expected to endure each other to the end of their days. These customs sound strange to Westerners oriented to romantic love, relative freedom of mate choice, and husband-wife companionship, but to the Chinese they were quite reasonable. The new wife was not seen as a romantic partner for her husband, but as a new recruit for the existing, corporate family. (In the great majority of cases the bride moved into her husband's family, rather than he moving into hers or the couple going off to start a new family of their own.) So it made perfect sense that the parents, rather than the young man, did the choosing. In fact, previous acquaintance and romantic involvement could create problems, since a groom too enamored of his bride would not show the required respect and obedience toward his parents, and might even respond to his bride's unhappiness by wanting to leave their home. If the bride was an intimidated stranger, her husband could be expected to fulfill his required role—to help bring her into line so that she would become a dutiful and deferential daughter-in-law, devoted to the interests of her new family.

Censure, Security, and Lack of Freedom

In sum, Chinese families in the past were characterized by an unusually strong sense of loyalty and obligation to a family unit that was seen as extending back many generations and that would persist long into the future—if family affairs were properly managed. Managing family affairs consisted of socializing family members into strict patterns of obedience and deference. To aid in this project, down through the ages literati and kin groups produced family advice manuals which laid down, sometimes in excruciating detail, the proper forms of behavior and family role obligations. If instruction failed, strict measures, including beatings and even expulsion, could be used against disobedient family members and the state generally approved of such harshness. These distinctive emphases in Chinese family life created strong family bonds and a sense of security as well as indebtedness; such sentiments could be a powerful force in motivating individuals to work hard, study diligently, and take risks—all for the welfare of the family. But these features were achieved at some cost, primarily in the unhappiness and frustrated aspirations of individual members whose needs and feelings might be overridden by the demands of the family and its patriarch.

Virtues of the Ideal Woman in Early Imperial China

Pan Chao

In imperial China, relations between the social classes, as well as between men and women, were based on the idea of harmony of differences rather than equality. Spouses had different but complementary roles based on the principle of yin and yang—yin representing the yielding or acquiescent nature of women and yang the more assertive and aggressive male nature. This differentiation did not imply that women were inferior, however. According to the teachings of Taoism, one of the major Chinese religions, softness and gentleness (yin) were often superior to hardness and rigidity (yang).

In the following article, Chinese historian Pan Chao (A.D. 48–112) provides a guide on how women should negotiate the new relationships they form when they marry and join their husbands' households. Chao draws on the concept of yin and yang to support her assertion that women should be modest, humble, amiable, and compliant. Chao, who served as a tutor to Empress Teng in 106, originally wrote the article as a guide for her daughters, whom she felt she may have neglected during her scholarly career. Her writing style demonstrates the humility that she contends should be a female virtue. Chao's guide became a respected text and, for the next several centuries, was seen as exemplifying the virtues of the ideal woman in imperial China.

I, the unworthy writer, am unsophisticated, unenlightened, and by nature unintelligent, but I am fortunate both to have received not a little favor from my scholarly father, and to have had a (cultured) mother and instructresses upon whom to rely for a literary education as well as for training in good manners. More than forty years have passed since at the age of fourteen I took up the dustpan and the broom in the Ts'ao family. During this time with trembling heart I feared constantly that I might disgrace my parents, and that I might multiply difficulties for both the women and the men (of my husband's family). Day and night I was distressed in heart, (but) I labored without confessing weariness. Now and hereafter, however, I know how to escape (from such fears).

Being careless, and by nature stupid, I taught and trained (my children) without system. Consequently I fear that my son Ku may bring disgrace upon the Imperial Dynasty by whose Holy Grace he has unprecedentedly received the extraordinary privilege of wearing the Gold and the Purple [of the Imperial officials] a privilege for the attainment of which (by my son, I) a humble subject never even hoped. Nevertheless, now that he is a man and able to plan his own life, I need not again have concern for him. But I do grieve that you, my daughters, just now at the age for marriage, have not at this time had gradual training and advice; that you still have not learned the proper customs for married women. I fear that by failure in good manners in other families you will humiliate both your ancestors and your clan. I am now seriously ill, life is uncertain. As I have thought of you all in so untrained a state, I have been uneasy many a time for you. At hours of leisure I have composed in seven chapters these instructions under the title, "Lessons for Women." In order that you may have something wherewith to benefit your persons, I wish every one of you, my daughters, each to write out a copy for yourself.

From this time on every one of you strive to practise these (lessons).

Chapter I Humility

On the third day after the birth of a girl the ancients observed three customs: (first) to place the baby below the bed; (second) to give her a potsherd [pottery fragment] with which to play; and (third) to announce her birth to her ancestors by an offering. Now to lay the baby below the bed plainly indicated that she is lowly and weak, and should regard it as her primary duty to humble herself before others. To give her potsherds with which to play indubitably signified that she should practise labor and consider it her primary duty to be industrious. To announce her birth before her ancestors clearly meant that she ought to esteem as her primary duty the continuation of the observance of worship in the home.

These three ancient customs epitomize a woman's ordinary way of life and the teachings of the traditional ceremonial rites and regulations. Let a woman modestly yield to others; let her respect others; let her put others first, herself last. Should she do something good, let her not mention it; should she do something bad, let her not deny it. Let her bear disgrace; let her even endure when others speak or do evil to her. Always let her seem to tremble and to fear. (When a woman follows such maxims as these,) then she may be said to humble herself before others.

Let a woman retire late to bed, but rise early to duties; let her not dread tasks by day or by night. Let her not refuse to perform domestic duties whether easy or difficult. That which must be done, let her finish completely, tidily, and systematically. (When a woman follows such rules as these,) then she may be said to be industrious.

Let a woman be correct in manner and upright in character in order to serve her husband. Let her live in purity and quietness (of spirit), and attend to her own affairs. Let her love not gossip and silly laughter. Let her cleanse and purify and arrange in order the wine and the food for the offerings to the ancestors. (When a woman observes such principles as these,) then she may be said to continue ancestral worship.

No woman who observes these three (fundamentals of life) has ever had a bad reputation or has fallen into disgrace. If a woman fails to observe them, how can her name be honored; how can she but bring disgrace upon herself?

Chapter II Husband and Wife

The Way of husband and wife is intimately connected with *Yin* and *Yang*, and relates the individual to gods and ancestors. Truly it is the great principle of Heaven and Earth, and the great basis of human relationships. Therefore the "Rites"[1] honor union of

---

1. Refers to the Book of Rites, one of five classical texts (including the Book of Poetry and the Book of Changes) held sacred by Confucius. Compiled during the Han dynasty (206 B.C.–A.D. 220), the Book of Rites set out rules for the conduct of Chinese rites and ceremonies.

man and woman; and in the "Book of Poetry" the "First Ode" manifests the principle of marriage. For these reasons the relationship cannot but be an important one.

If a husband be unworthy, then he possesses nothing by which to control his wife. If a wife be unworthy, then she possesses nothing with which to serve her husband. If a husband does not control his wife, then the rules of conduct manifesting his authority are abandoned and broken. If a wife does not serve her husband, then the proper relationship (between men and women) and the natural order of things are neglected and destroyed. As a matter of fact the purpose of these two (the controlling of women by men, and the serving of men by women) is the same.

Now examine the gentlemen of the present age. They only know that wives must be controlled, and that the husband's rules of conduct manifesting his authority must be established. They therefore teach their boys to read books and (study) histories. But they do not in the least understand that husbands and masters must (also) be served, and that the proper relationship and the rites should be maintained.

Yet only to teach men and not to teach women,—is that not ignoring the essential relation between them? According to the "Rites," it is the rule to begin to teach children to read at the age of eight years, and by the age of fifteen years they ought then to be ready for cultural training. Only why should it not be (that girls' education as well as boys' be) according to this principle?

Chapter III Respect and Caution

As *Yin* and *Yang* are not of the same nature, so man and woman have different characteristics. The distinctive quality of the *Yang* is rigidity; the function of the *Yin* is yielding. Man is honored for strength; a woman is beautiful on account of her gentleness. Hence there arose the common saying: "A man though born like a wolf may, it is feared, become a weak monstrosity; a woman though born like a mouse may, it is feared, become a tiger."

Now for self-culture nothing equals respect for others. To counteract firmness nothing equals compliance. Consequently it can be said that the Way of respect and acquiescence is woman's most important principle of conduct. So respect may be defined as nothing other than holding on to that which is permanent; and acquiescence nothing other than being liberal and generous. Those who are steadfast in devotion know that they should stay in their proper places; those who are liberal and generous esteem others, and honor and serve (them).

If husband and wife have the habit of staying together, never leaving one another, and following each other around within the limited space of their own rooms, then they will lust after and take liberties with one another. From such action improper language will arise between the two. This kind of discussion may lead to licentiousness. Out of licentiousness will be born a heart of disrespect to the husband. Such a result comes from not knowing that one should stay in one's proper place.

Furthermore, affairs may be either crooked or straight; words may be either right or wrong. Straightforwardness cannot but lead to quarreling; crookedness cannot but lead to accusation. If there are really accusations and quarrels, then undoubtedly there will be angry affairs. Such a result comes from not esteeming others, and not honoring and serving (them).

(If wives) suppress not contempt for husbands, then it follows (that such wives) rebuke and scold (their husbands). (If husbands) stop not short of anger, then they are certain to beat (their wives). The correct relationship between husband and wife is based upon harmony and intimacy, and (conjugal) love is grounded in proper union. Should actual blows be dealt, how could matrimonial relationship be preserved? Should sharp words be spoken, how could (conjugal) love exist? If love and proper relationship both be destroyed, then husband and wife are divided.

Chapter IV Womanly Qualifications

A woman (ought to) have four qualifications: (1) womanly virtue; (2) womanly words; (3) womanly bearing; and (4) womanly work. Now what is called womanly virtue need not be brilliant ability, exceptionally different from others. Womanly words need be neither clever in debate nor keen in conversation. Womanly appearance requires neither a pretty nor a perfect face and form. Womanly work need not be work done more skillfully than that of others.

To guard carefully her chastity; to control circumspectly her behavior; in every motion to exhibit modesty; and to model each act on the best usage, this is womanly virtue.

To choose her words with care; to avoid vulgar language; to speak at appropriate times; and not to weary others (with much conversation), may be called the characteristics of womanly words.

To wash and scrub filth away; to keep clothes and ornaments fresh and clean; to wash the head and bathe the body regularly, and to keep the person free from disgraceful filth, may be called the characteristics of womanly bearing.

With whole-hearted devotion to sew and to weave; to love not gossip and silly laughter; in cleanliness and order (to prepare) the wine and food for serving guests, may be called the characteristics of womanly work.

These four qualifications characterize the greatest virtue of a woman. No woman can afford to be without them. In fact they are very easy to possess if a woman only treasure them in her heart. The ancients had a saying: "Is Love afar off? If I desire love, then love is at hand!" So can it be said of these qualifications.

Chapter V Whole-Hearted Devotion

Now in the "Rites" is written the principle that a husband may marry again, but there is no Canon that authorizes a woman to be married the second time. Therefore it is said of husbands as of Heaven, that as certainly as people cannot run away from Heaven, so surely a wife cannot leave (a husband's home).

If people in action or character disobey the spirits of Heaven and of Earth, then Heaven punishes them. Likewise if a woman errs in the rites and in the proper mode of conduct, then her husband esteems her lightly. The ancient book, "A Pattern for Women" (Nü Hsien), says: "To obtain the love of one man is the crown of a woman's life; to lose the love of one man is to miss the aim in woman's life." For these reasons a woman cannot but seek to win her husband's heart. Nevertheless, the beseeching wife need not use flattery, coaxing words, and cheap methods to gain intimacy.

Decidedly nothing is better (to gain the heart of a husband) than whole-hearted devotion and correct manners. In accor-

Foot Binding

Foot binding began as a practice of the upper classes during the Song dynasty (960–1279) and continued until the early twentieth century. At the age of seven or eight, girls had their feet tightly wrapped and slowly bent until the arches were broken and their toes turned under. If all went well, they emerged with feet that were three or four inches long, which was considered a sign of feminine beauty. Historian Dorothy Ko describes the foot binding ritual.

The ritual of footbinding, an exclusively female affair, reinforced the ideal and practice of separate male/female domains. Long before the binding started, a girl's mother would prepare the various implements needed. Besides alum, an astringent, these were either implements already in use in the women's world—scissors, nail clippers, needle, and thread—or made for the occasion by the elder women in the house. A sample checklist reads: a bandage ten centimeters wide and ten meters long, lightly starched and free of wrinkles; five pairs of cloth shoes with flat bottoms; three pairs of cloth slippers for bed; several pairs of tight socks. . . .

A central event in the domestic women's culture, the process of footbinding was often launched with a prayer to the gods. A Ming [dynasty (1368–1644)] household almanac . . . stipulated rules for picking auspicious days to inaugurate this rite of passage. In Suzhou [a major city in Southern China], binding customarily started on the twenty-fourth day of the eight month, when the Tiny-Foot Maiden (Xiaojiao Guniang), the deity in charge of footbinding, enjoyed of-

dance with the rites and the proper mode of conduct, (let a woman) live a pure life. Let her have ears that hear not licentiousness; and eyes that see not depravity. When she goes outside her own home, let her not be conspicuous in dress and manners. When at home let her not neglect her dress. Women should not assemble in groups, nor gather together, (for gossip and silly laughter). They should not stand watching in the gateways. (If a woman follows) these rules, she may be said to have wholehearted devotion and correct manners.

If, in all her actions, she is frivolous, she sees and hears (only) that which pleases herself. At home her hair is dishevelled, and her dress is slovenly. Outside the home she emphasizes her femininity to attract attention; she says what ought not to be said; and she looks at what ought not to be seen. (If a woman does ferings from her devotees. On that day, girls shaped rice balls from glutinous rice and red beans, praying that their bones would be just as soft. . . .

These female-exclusive rituals and the beliefs behind them help explain the longevity and spread of the custom. For all its erotic appeal to men, without the cooperation of the women concerned, footbinding could not have been perpetuated for a millennium. In defining the mother-daughter tie in a private space barred to men, in venerating the fruits of women's handiwork, and in the centrality of female-exclusive religious rituals, footbinding embodied the essential features of a women's culture documented by the writings of the women themselves. . . . Throughout a woman's life, fascination with the foot continued to be a central motif in her interaction with other women. Women exchanged poems eulogizing small feet; mementos such as embroidered shoes were as widely used as poems in cementing female friendships.

In this lies the ambivalent nature of a woman's self-identity and women's culture in seventeenth-century China. On a negative note, women seemed to have accepted without question a philosophical and ethical tradition predicated on their confinement. In the seventeenth century, they had yet to question the premise of that tradition, nor did they raise objections in a concerted voice. On a positive note, they managed to create a meaningful and colorful world of their own within the constraints of their historical time and space.

Dorothy Ko, *Teachers of the Inner Chambers*. Stanford, CA: Stanford University Press, 1994.

such as) these, (she may be) said to be without whole-hearted devotion and correct manners.

Chapter VI Implicit Obedience

Now "to win the love of one man is the crown of a woman's life; to lose the love of one man is her eternal disgrace." This saying advises a fixed will and a whole-hearted devotion for a woman. Ought she then to lose the hearts of her father- and mother-in-law?

There are times when love may lead to differences of opinion (between individuals); there are times when duty may lead to disagreement. Even should the husband say that he loves something, when the parents-in-law say "no," this is called a case of duty leading to disagreement. This being so, then what about the hearts of the parents-in-law? Nothing is better than an obedience which sacrifices personal opinion.

Whenever the mother-in-law says, "Do not do that," and if what she says is right, unquestionably the daughter-in-law obeys. Whenever the mother-in-law says, "Do that," even if what she says is wrong, still the daughter-in-law submits unfailingly to the command.

Let a woman not act contrary to the wishes and the opinions of parents-in-law about right and wrong; let her not dispute with them what is straight and what is crooked. Such (docility) may be called obedience which sacrifices personal opinion. Therefore the ancient book, "A Pattern for Women," says: "If a daughter-in-law (who follows the wishes of her parents-in-law) is like an echo and a shadow, how could she not be praised?"

Housing and Clothing at the Height of the Imperial Age

Jacques Gernet

In the final years of the Southern Song dynasty in the thirteenth century, imperial China was at the height of its glory, and Hangzhou (Hangchow), the capital, was the largest and richest city in the empire, with the most culturally and technologically advanced society in the world. In the following extract from *Daily Life in China on the Eve of the Mongol Invasion, 1250–1276*, French scholar Jacques Gernet contrasts the crowded living quarters of the poor with the resplendent homes of high officials and the lavish lifestyle of the emperor. His description of clothing worn by Hangzhou's inhabitants also underscores the disparities between rich and poor. He suggests that official regulation of dress style, headgear, and footwear was designed to preserve the rigid social hierarchy of imperial China. Gernet relied almost completely on original Chinese texts for the information in his book. He has written many titles on Chinese history and culture, including *A History of Chinese Civilization* (1995) and *Buddhism in Chinese Society* (1998).

Not all the inhabitants of Hangchow were fortunate enough to have a roof over their heads. Beggars and penniless wretches slept in the open, and, since overcrowding was often exacerbated by the frequent fires which ravaged the city, others were always having to be provided with temporary accommodation. The cells and courtyards of monasteries, boats on the lake, military barracks and hastily erected shelters made of waterproof matting were put at the disposal of homeless families and of victims of disasters. One section of the population lived permanently on the boats on the canals—the boatmen and their families.

Jacques Gernet, *Daily Life in China on the Eve of the Mongol Invasion, 1250–1276*. Stanford, CA: Stanford University Press, 1962.

As for those people of the lower classes who did have some-
where to live, they had to crowd six or seven together, possibly
more, in one tiny room. In spite of the multi-storeyed houses in
the poorer districts, there were too many people for the available
accommodation in a town squeezed between the river and the
lake. Streets, markets and houses overflowed with people. . . .

The basic materials were wood and bamboo brought by boat
from the region south of Hangchow, and bricks and tiles. . . .

Construction Techniques

Houses for the rich and houses for the poor, edifices and temples,
whether public or private, were all built by the same methods.
The main structure did not consist of foundations and bearer-
walls, but of wooden pillars spaced about three yards apart, resting on stone supports sunk ten to twenty inches in the ground.
The size of a house, or of a covered arcade or a gateway, was
reckoned in the number of spaces between priors, or, as one
might say, in spans. The lightness and rigidity of the whole structure meant that it could be raised from the base, so that the entire building could be moved elsewhere if necessary.

All buildings, without exception, were rectangular in shape;
they were sometimes subdivided across their width by one or
two partitions. As many constructions of its kind as might be required were scattered about the parks and gardens of the rich,
either set at right angles to each other to form a U enclosing a
courtyard, or else separate. They had a ground floor only, or one
storey at the most. In the poorer districts, on the other hand, the
houses formed an uninterrupted façade along the lanes. Joined
one to another and extending in depth, they no doubt gave on
to small courtyards at the back. Many of them consisted of several storeys, if the accounts of [Venetian traveler] Marco Polo and
of Arab and European travellers of the fourteenth century are to
be believed. . . .

Roofs and Ornaments

The roof, the most important and the most expensive item in
house-building, was put on as soon as the pillars for supporting
it were in place. It always had two slopes, and rested on a com-
bination of mainbeams and crossbeams, and sometimes on ex-

terior brackets as well, which, in the finest buildings, gave an effect of a roof detached from the rest of the building and floating in the air. The parts of the roof-timbers exposed to view were adorned with carvings and painted in bright colours. The finest roofs, with tiles glazed yellow, pale green or jade-green, and with slightly upturned edges, harmonized to perfection with near-by trees and with the varied curves of the hills surrounding the lake.

The custom of making roofs with upturned edges was probably fairly recent in the thirteenth century. It cannot have become widespread until the T'ang dynasty (seventh to tenth century), and the method of obtaining the required curves was still rather clumsy at that time. An architect of the eleventh century who wrote an important treatise on the rules of his art, and who invites us to share his admiration for the builders of the T'ang period, adds that they were not very skilled in curving the edges of their roofs upwards. It is worth noting, incidentally, that curved roofs were reserved, by imperial decree, for the houses of people of high rank and for government buildings. As for constructing roofs for shops and ordinary houses, no one would have thought of spending money on such a costly method

Similarly, ornaments in the form of aigrettes and small terracotta animals, dragons and phoenixes, which were to be seen on the ridge and eaves of roofs on the houses of nobles and officials as well as on government buildings, were forbidden to the common people. . . .

Houses of the Rich and the Poor

The houses in the poorer districts gave directly on to the street, unless there was a courtyard in between. In either case, shops, restaurants and small workrooms were always on the ground floor. These houses with fronts open on to the street were no doubt typical of all the towns of South China, and gave Hangchow a friendly air which the capitals of T'ang times with their houses closed in on themselves and their districts shut off with walls of dry earth, had never known, except perhaps in a few of the busiest streets. The blind walls along the lanes in present-day Peking [Beijing] probably give a fairly good idea of the appearance presented by the residential quarters of the great cities of the North in T'ang times. But walls of this kind, with no openings other than doors, were also to be found in some parts of Hangchow in the thirteenth century. They hid from view official buildings, temples, palaces, monasteries, and the residences of important people, high officials and rich merchants.

Behind them were tall single-storeyed buildings with roofs extending into porches, dwelling-houses with courtyards surrounded by covered arcades, and detached two-storeyed buildings and small summer-houses scattered among trees and flower-gardens. The main residential quarters of wealthy establishments consisted of a group of buildings set at right angles or placed parallel to each other, separated by a series of courtyards varying in number. The ground-level of the buildings was slightly higher than that of the courtyards, and the main hall was reached by several steps placed in the centre of the building. The front gate leading into the first courtyard was a square structure, also above ground-level, which was roofed. It served as shelter for the gatekeepers. Sumptuary regulations [government rules

Sung Dynasty
(A.D. 960–1279)

Hangchow

The Great Wall

Present-day
boundary of China

Northern Sung Dynasty
(A.D. 960–1127)

Southern Sung Dynasty
(A.D. 1127–1279)

to preserve the social hierarchy] did not allow private persons to have gates more than one span wide. Only important dignitaries of the empire might have gates with several passageways, such as were to be seen at the Imperial Palace. Gates had a screen in front of them consisting of a wall six feet high which hid the entrance and was supposed to keep out baleful influences. We might mention here another form of protection against bad luck and demons: the gate gods. Painted images of them were placed one on each side of the gateway to prevent evil spirits from entering the house. These gods were historical persons who had been deified—two captains of the guard who, according to the legend, kept armed guard at the door of the apartments of the first T'ang emperor and thus put an end to his nightmares.

The group of buildings composing the residential quarters of the finest houses, with their upturned roofs and porches one behind the other and their long covered arcades, presented a total effect that was most harmonious. But each single one of the detached buildings was designed to produce some special picturesque effect. Each pavilion was built for a particular purpose: perhaps one from which the moonlight could be admired, another for music-making, another for banquets, yet another, set in the shade of bamboos and pines and hung with paintings of snow scenes inside, for keeping cool in hot weather. Sometimes summer-houses were built on piles over an artificial pool which could be reached by boat or by a little wooden bridge. It was said that many wealthy people had spent a fortune on constructing and making improvements to their residences. Sometimes rare woods, aloe and sandalwood, imported from tropical countries, were used for the pillars and framework. The floor was often paved with glazed bricks, and there is even one case cited of a rich man who had his floor inlaid with a floral design in silver.

Ornate Gardens

Just as much thought was given to gardens and artificial pools as to the actual buildings. It was the harmonious lines of the total effect that was considered important. A poet of T'ang times recommended that, for a well-planned residence, a sixth of the total area should be assigned to the house, half to lakes and ponds, and a third to plantations of bamboos. The natural scenery of these gardens was all man-made: little artificial hills, winding streams with waterfalls, ponds in which swam those gold and silver fishes that were sold in the town under the name of 'long-life fishes' and were reared in large quantities outside one of the north-west gates.

No fine house was without its rare flowers or without pine-trees with gnarled trunks and twisted branches; no good garden without the curious stones it was then the fashion to collect. These rocks worn by wind or water were like miniature mountains. Sometimes they were placed so as to represent one of the famous sites where Taoist immortals were supposed to dwell. Planted perhaps with dwarf trees (probably already used at that time), pierced with little grottoes where perfumes could be burnt to make smoke that looked like clouds, and with little lakes here and there, these curious rocks invited ecstatic excursions. Those who delighted in them, shrunk, as sometimes happens to immortals, to dimensions in accord with the little paths and tracks that wound about these mountains in miniature, could wander freely there in imagination. This is a particular form of expression of the Chinese aesthetic sense which comes from an ancient magical conception of the art of representation, and which is also to be found in the landscape painting and in the art of landscape gardening. Gardens were sometimes laid out to represent some famous mountain site. Wandering there, one derived strength from contact with its strange stones, ancient trees and rare plants, and, as one contemplated the fish darting capriciously hither and thither, a sense of renewal from the feeling of natural spontaneity which the scene conveyed.

Imperial Palace

Marco Polo's description of the Imperial Palace deserves to be quoted in its entirety, because it is full of interesting details about the imperial residence, which formed a small walled city of its town. . . .

> Now we will speak of a most beautiful palace where the King Fanfur [who governed South China until defeated by Kublai Khan in 1269] lived, whose predecessors had had a space of country enclosed which they surrounded for ten miles with very high walls and divided it into three parts. In the middle part one en-

tered through a very large gate, where were found on one side and on the other very large and broad pavilions on the level ground, with the roof supported by columns which were painted and worked with gold and the finest azures. Then at the head was seen the principal one and larger than all the others, painted in the like way with the pillars gilt, and the ceiling with the most beautiful ornaments of gold; and round about on the walls the stories of the past kings were painted with the greatest skill. There every year on certain days dedicated to his idols the King Fanfur used to hold court and give a banquet to the chief lords, great masters, and rich artificers of the city of Quinsai [in southern China] and ten thousand persons at one time sat at table there conveniently under all the said pavilions. And this court lasted ten or twelve days, and it was a stupendous thing and past all belief to see the magnificence of the guests dressed in silk and in gold with so many precious stones upon them, because each one did his utmost to go with the greatest display and wealth in his power. Behind this pavilion of which we have spoken, which was entered through the middle of the great gate, there was a wall with a door which divided off the other part of the palace, where on entering one found another great place made in the manner of a cloister with its pillars which held up the portico which went round the said cloister, and there were various rooms for the king and queen which were likewise worked with various works, and so were all the walls. Then from this cloister one entered into a walk six paces wide, all covered; but it was so long that it reached down to the lake. On this walk ten courts on one side and ten on the other stood facing one another, fashioned like long cloisters with their porticoes all round, and each cloister or court had fifty rooms with their gardens, and in all these rooms were stationed a thousand girls whom the king kept for his service. And sometimes he went with the queen and with some of the said [girls] for recreation about the lake on barges all covered with silk, and also to visit the temples of the idols. The other two parts of the said enclosure were laid out with woods, lakes, and most beautiful gardens planted with fruit trees, where were enclosed all sorts of animals, that is roe-deer, fallow-deer, red-deer, hares, rabbits; and there the king went to enjoy himself with his damsels, some in carriages and some on horseback, and no man went in there. And he made the said [damsels] run with dogs and give chase to these kinds of animals; and after they were tired they went into these woods which faced one another above the said lakes, and leaving the clothes there they came out of them naked and entered into the water and set themselves to swim some on one side and some on the other, and the king stayed to watch them with

the greatest delight; and then they went back home. Sometimes
he had food carried into these woods, which were thick and dense
with very lofty trees, waited on by the said damsels. . . .

Clothing and Social Standing

It was commonly held in China that the essential function of
clothing was protection from the cold. Certainly, methods of
heating were rudimentary even in the houses of wealthy people
and were practically non-existent among the poor in south-east
China. Coal was scarce and expensive. Hence the main protection against intense cold was clothing lined with floss silk and
fur-lined coats. But clothing was also one of the obvious signs of
social standing. Among the ruling class, clothing was just as
much an indication of rank as were insignia of various kinds or
the number and style of one's retinue. The colour and orna-
mentation of the dress to be worn, the shape and type of headgear, the particular style of girdle—all such details were laid
down, for every occasion and for each grade of the hierachy, by
imperial decree, in fulfilment of ritual requirements.

The official histories contain monographs entirely devoted to
describing in the minutest detail the costumes, headgear, girdles,
carriages and seals of the Emperor, of his close kin, and of high
dignitaries of the court and other officials. A large number of de-
crees were concerned with questions of this kind which to us
moderns seem of minor importance. Not so to the Chinese of
those times, for the regulation of ceremonial details had the double purpose of keeping a check on expenditure and of producing
a desired psychological effect. The regulations perpetuated the
age-old attachment to the outward signs of prestige, and,
through the very importance attributed to them, they in turn
aroused appropriate emotions. According to the Chinese expression, their purpose was to bring the outward and the inward
into harmony with each other. In order to believe, there is nothing better than to begin by wholeheartedly complying with the
ritual gestures performed by believers: faith will then come of itself and without the asking, In our day, only the army, with its
ranks, its uniforms and its rituals, can help us to understand the
traditional Chinese world, the purest manifestation of which was
to be found in T'ang times.

At the beginning of the Sung dynasty, towards the end of the tenth century, there was still a series of colours prescribed for each grade in the hierarchy of the mandarinate: above the third degree, robes must be purple; above the sixth, vermilion; above the seventh, green; above the ninth, turquoise. Black and white were only worn by ordinary individuals. However these regulations soon fell into disuse, because the court granted the right to wear purple indiscriminately to officials of all grades.

The same thing happened with the round parasols of bluegreen silk which in the first instance had been reserved for princes of

---

The Chinese Practice of Feng Shui

In designing houses or cities, the Chinese in the imperial age would call on geomancers, or feng shui specialists, to give advice on the most auspicious design and placement of buildings, houses, rooms, and even articles of furniture. Scholar Michael Loewe describes the principles underlying the Chinese practice of feng shui.

[Underlying] the ancient Chinese art of *feng-shui*, or geomancy . . . was the belief that invisible forces (*qi:* breaths, vapors, energies) control nature and the destiny of people. They flow above and below [the earth]. Human activities, such as digging and building, disrupt, obstruct, and injure the currents. As a result, natural disasters occur and, more important, one's luck takes a turn for the worse. In the early seventh century a Sui [dynasty, 581–617] official observed that a large lake southwest of Changan [in central China] was exerting an adverse effect on the capital, and suggested that the erection of a pagoda could counter its influence. In geomancy, water, the element of yin (the moon, dark, pliant, female) could exert either a benevolent or a malevolent force on the site of a city, dwelling, or grave, depending on its location and character. A river with a slow current that flowed south and turned to the east was a benign influence. In this case the lake was to the west and was not flowing at all. Therefore, it was stagnant and lifeless. To remedy such a situation, geomancers usually proposed interposing a tall object, often a tree for a home, that represented yang (the sun, light, rigid, fire, male) between the structure and the water. A pagoda was ideal for a city, given its height. So in 611 the emperor had a pagoda built of wood that was 330 feet tall and 120 paces in circumference at the southwest corner of Changan.

Michael Loewe, *Everyday Life in Early Imperial China During the Han Period, 202 B.C.–A.D. 220.* New York: Dorset Press, 1968.

the imperial family. From the end of the tenth century permission was granted to certain officials to carry these parasols; then it was granted to women of the palace when they paid visits to town. . . .

Distinctive Clothing

It was by their costume that, at first glance, people of rank and *nouveau-riche* merchants could be distinguished from the common people in the streets of Hangchow. The former wore a long robe that reached down to the ground, the latter a blouse that came down below the waist and trousers made of light-coloured material. The women wore either long dresses, or blouses which came down nearly as far as the knee, jackets with long or short sleeves, and skirts. When they went walking in the streets, women and young girls sometimes threw over their shoulders a square scarf, purple in colour, which was called a 'head-cover'. As distinguished from men, their clothes were fastened on the left side and not on the right. Men of rank had self-coloured robes for everyday wear, and robes with symbolic designs embroidered on them for ceremonial occasions: phoenixes, dragons, or birds with lucky plants held in their beaks. The fastenings were the same as those used in [twentieth-century] Chinese dress: little oblong buttons fastened by loops of cloth. Robes were often edged with cloth of a deeper colour round the neck and sleeves. The sleeves, which had very wide openings, could be used for carrying small articles in them. . . .

Footwear and Headgear

Footwear of many kinds was to be found in Hangchow: leather shoes sold under the name of 'oiled footwear', wooden or hempen sandals, satin slippers. Grand people went about perched on buskins of a sort, to make them taller. No one ever went about barefoot, just as no one ever went bareheaded. Even the very poorest were shod and wore some kind of headgear, and it was only Buddhist monks who went about the streets with their shaved heads unprotected by any kind of covering.

But it was never a cap or a hat that the women wore. Their headwear was confined to hairpins and combs stuck into their hair, which was always most artistically arranged. Ladies of rank, princesses and imperial concubines, officials' ladies and the wives of rich merchants, also wore head ornaments in gold and silver wrought in the form of phoenixes and flowers. Archaeological excavations have unearthed several specimens of pieces of jewellery of this kind and revealed their exquisite workmanship. The phoenix ornaments, placed one on each side of the head, rose up like two wings and hid the hair almost completely. Ladies also wore chignon rings and ear-rings. This love of head ornaments which was so much in vogue in Hangchow had already existed and been remarked upon by Arab travellers in the ninth century. 'The women,' says one Arab account, 'go about with head uncovered and put combs in their hair. Sometimes a woman will wear as many as twenty combs made of ivory and other materials.' But instead of having the hair piled up high on the forehead as had been the fashion in Tang times, women now wore it combed back and gathered into a chignon.

Servant girls could be recognized by the peculiar style in which their hair was worn: it was brought forward to the front of the head and tied into two tufts by ribbons of many colours, and a fringe was worn on the forehead.

Most men were cleanshaven, but a few wore long side-whiskers and a goatee beard, particularly military men: it was a sign of virility to have a vigorous growth of hair. Hence the soldiers who were boxing champions wore side-whiskers and beards and long hair hanging down to their shoulders. As for children, their heads were shaved, leaving only a small tuft on top at the front.

The men of the ruling class wore a great variety of headgear, each with a different name. But it was the Emperor whose wardrobe was particularly rich in headwear of all kinds designed for special ceremonial occasions. One of them consisted of a cap surmounted by a horizontal board from which hung twelve pendants. Most headgear was made of black silk. The kind of cap usually worn by the scholars covered the hair completely and was tied behind by two ends which stuck out like two long, rather stiff ears. Some people defied ridicule and wore caps in antique style, and there were shops that specialized in old-fashioned headgear of this kind. As for the common people, they usually wore turbans of a sort. It was still possible in Hangchow, as it bad been in Kaifeng at the beginning of the twelfth century, to recognize a man's trade from the shape and colour of his turban. But there were other types of headgear as well: round straw hats for wearing in the rain, and hats made of leather.

Girdles

Another essential article of clothing, as well as headgear of some sort, was the girdle: these were the two things which distinguished the Chinese from the barbarian. The girdle, which very often was an article of value, was always worn, both with a robe and with a blouse. The finest girdles had plaques or buckles in jade, in gold, or in rhinoceros horn. The horn was imported from India, and in particular from Bengal, which was supposed to have the best horn. This was an old luxury trade, and had for long been in the hands of Persian and Arab merchants. 'The Chinese,' says an Arab account of the ninth century, 'make from this horn girdles which fetch a price of two or three thousand dinars or more. . . .' The astonishing prices fetched by these horns and the intense delight taken by Chinese in ornaments made from them can hardly be explained by their rarity-value alone: superstition as well as artistic taste must lie at the root of this passion. And indeed we find that [according to French author J. Sauvage] 'sometimes the horn is in the image of a man, or a peacock, or a fish, or some other thing.' The more unusual and handsome the image, the higher the price of the horn. For it was also a kind of talisman. Other girdles were ornamented with plaques of jade, gold, bronze or iron. This article of apparel also had its official regulations, which, at the end of the tenth century, laid down what type of girdle was to be worn by each grade in the hierarchy.

Elementary Education in Late Imperial China

Angela Ki Che Leung

Although formal education was restricted to the upper classes for most of the imperial age, the Chinese placed great store on transmitting the wisdom of the great sages. Knowledge of the classics, which outlined each citizen's duties and obligations to his or her family members and other social groups, was seen as the key to social harmony. The educational system aimed to produce orderly members of society who fulfilled the duties and obligations required of all the emperor's subjects. Parents of upper-class families sought to advance their children's education to maintain or improve their social standing, and the state promoted education to ensure an adequate supply of officials.

In the following extract, historian Angela Ki Che Leung describes the methods and content of school education for children six to fifteen years of age in the Ming and early Qing periods of the seventeenth and eighteenth centuries. Her study centers on education in the lower Yangtze area of China, which was then the richest and among the most culturally advanced regions of the country. Leung describes the typical school day, exploring how reading and writing were taught, how children were disciplined, and how moral values were imparted.

Angela Ki Che Leung, who specializes in imperial Chinese sociocultural history, is a research fellow at the Sun Yat-sen Institute of Social Sciences and Philosophy in Taiwan. Her recent books include *Charity and Moral Transformation: Philanthropic Organization of the Ming and Qing Periods* (1997).

T he ideal school calendar corresponded to the natural year and began around the fifteenth of the first month and ended around the twenty-fifth of the twelfth month with a total of about

Angela Ki Che Leung, "Elementary Education in the Lower Yangtze Region in the Seventeenth and Eighteenth Centuries," *Education and Society in Late Imperial China, 1600–1900,* edited by Benjamin A. Elman and Alexander Woodside. Berkeley: University of California Press, 1994.

ten days off for the celebration of various festivals. A complete school year consisted of eleven full months. Not only was the year rather long but the school day also lasted practically from sunup to sundown. A typical schedule consisted of four parts: the early morning session held before breakfast, the morning session after breakfast, the afternoon session, and a brief evening session. Clearly, the school calendar and the daily schedule reflected notions of time natural to an essentially agrarian society.

The schools accepted children between the ages of about eight to fifteen *sui* [years], even though it is likely that some younger children, who had been taught a number of characters at home, started school earlier at six or seven. There was no yearly program governing the progress of learning of the children during the seven or so years they spent in the school. There seemed to be a tacit agreement among educators that children be taught according to their indiviual aptitudes [according to the educator Liu Tsung-chou (1578–1645)]. "Teaching should not be uniform for everybody." One can thus imagine that children from six or seven to about fifteen were taught together in the same class while the teacher, if he was a responsible one, had to attend to each pupil's individual progress and give him suitable guidance. This explains the small number of pupils in an ideal typical primary school. . . .

Reading and Writing

Contrary to what many may think, the first years of elementary education, at least in the seventeenth and eighteenth centuries, were not particularly trying: the child could apparently learn at his own pace. Except for those who entered school already knowing some characters, the first thing to be learned in school was to recognize characters and to review them regularly after they were taught. There seemed to be different methods of teaching characters to children. Besides the classical way (since Sung times) of recognizing and memorizing characters in the three major primers—the *Trimetrical Classic* (*San-tzu ching*), the *Thousand Character Classic* (*Ch'ien tzu wen*), and the *Hundred Surnames* (*Pai chia hsing*)—characters were also taught separately on paper or wooden squares. One character was written on each square and a child was taught to recognize some ten characters a day; the memorized characters were tied with a string and these were reviewed constantly while new ones were being taught. There was general agreement that a child should know between one and two thousand characters before he was taught to read a text. Thereafter, difficult new characters that appeared in texts were singled out and posted up by the teacher every day. The pupils learned to recognize these as they proceeded on to different texts. Again, there was no precise rule on the time to be spent on this phase of preliminary learning: everything depended on the ability of the child.

Writing with the brush began slightly later than, or at the same time as this first phase. The teacher had to hold the hand of the pupil to show him the correct way to hold the brush and to draw a character before he was permitted to write on his own. These beginners were only allowed to write simple, big characters by imitating popular models of the standard script (*cheng-k'ai*). The first characters written were not exactly the same as the thousand or so characters in the primers that the child had now recognized. (Most of these were too complicated to be drawn at this early stage). Small characters could be practiced only after the child could handle the big ones with ease. Writing

Building Mathematics Skills in Early Imperial China

Mathematics textbooks for students in the second century B.C. had exercises that resemble the types of tests given to students more than two thousand years later. One such text posed the following problem.

A fast horse and a slow horse set out together on the 3000 *li* [550 miles] long journey from Ch'ang-an to Ch'i. The first day the fast horse travels 193 *li*, thereafter increasing his speed by 13 *li* each day. The slow horse covers 97 *li* on the first day, thereafter reducing his speed by ½ *li* each day. After reaching Ch'i the fast horse starts his return journey and meets the slow horse. When does the meeting take place and how far has each horse travelled? . . .

The answers thoughtfully provided in the textbook are as follows: after $15^{135}/_{191}$ days, the fast horse has travelled $4534^{46}/_{191}$ *li*, and the slow horse $1465^{145}/_{191}$ *li*.

Quoted in Michael Loewe, *Everyday Life in Early Imperial China During the Han Period, 202 B.C.–A.D. 220.* New York: Dorset Press, 1968.

was practiced every day during the second morning session and the teacher marked each well- and badly written character in order to encourage or to correct the child.

Besides the three classical primers that almost all children learned to recite during their first years in school, there were other textbooks that the child started to learn as soon as he had acquired a sufficient number of characters to read them. These texts contained knowledge of all kinds and were written in song or poetic form to make them more interesting and easier for the child to memorize. . . .

At the same time, some children started to learn some of the standard texts. Almost every teacher found it necessary at one time or at another to teach the Four Books and some of the Five Classics [main texts of Confucianism], which were to be learned by heart by the children as soon as they could recognize some one thousand or so characters. On methods of teaching this core material, however, there seemed to be slight differences among educators. For some, the child was receptive enough at eight or nine to understand the teaching of the Classics. Thus, the teacher had to explain the texts to the child before he could memorize them in order to "stimulate his intelligence." According to the late Ming scholar Liu Tsung-chou (1578–1645, native of Shan-yin, Chekiang), every text was to be explained word by word, phrase by phrase before the overall meaning was explicated. The moral content of the texts received particular emphasis. In contrast, other authorities believed children of this age could not possibly understand the true meaning of the Classics: "Children only use their mouths and their ears, and not their hearts and their eyes . . ."; "children before they are fifteen can memorize better than they understand . . . and they can understand better and memorize less after they are fifteen." However, whatever the teachers' conceptions of a child's learning ability at this early stage, they all agreed on one essential aspect of the learning of the Classics, which is also the best-known characteristic of classical primary education: drilling and rote memory.

One of the typical ways of drilling a child was provided by the experienced primary teacher Ch'en Fang-sheng:

> Texts well-memorized during childhood will be remembered the whole life. For every new text one learns each day, one has to re-

vise ten old texts. The new text has to be read aloud one hundred times, after which one has to revise the old texts according to the order in which they have been learned. A fixed number of pages have to be revised every day. When they are finished, they have to be revised all over again. At the beginning page of the text, one has to mark the day when the text is first revised; at the end of the text, one has to mark the day when the study of the text is completed. . . . [The teacher] has to make a list of the texts that each pupil has learned and stick it on the right side of his seat; each time the pupil has finished revising a text, the teacher will mark a circle against the title of the text in red ink.

Indeed, a child was considered intelligent only if he could quickly memorize a great quantity of texts. All educators recommended that all reading aloud and recitation of previously learned texts be done in the first morning session, probably because the children's minds were at their freshest then. The explanation and reading aloud of new texts, on the other hand, were done in the second morning session. . . .

Teaching Morals and Values

For scholastic curricula of all kinds and all times, it is always difficult to distinguish between the practical knowledge they transmit and the set of values they try to convey.

All the texts mentioned above, even the more difficult Classics, had the practical function of teaching new characters to the pupils. Some of the primers taught them history, geography, important cultural references, names of tools and utensils, common plants and animals, social rules, and so on, all of which were useful knowledge for daily functioning in Ming-Ch'ing society: for reading notices and family handbooks (*lei-shu*), for writing official letters and other documents, for keeping accounts and recording simple business transactions, and for enjoying theatrical performances and popular novels. But more was taught by these same texts during the same process: the worldview common to the average Chinese of the time, common notions of time and space, and a shared set of values. For many educators, this, more than the practical learning, was the main purpose of elementary education.

Indeed, as [Chinese poet] Ch'en Ch'ueh put it, the elementary education that one gave to a child of six or seven and above "should first teach him how to follow rites and manners, the most fundamental of which is to let him know what are filial piety and respect. Let him practice loyalty and honesty; reading and writing come only in second place." Li Chao-lo [nineteenth-century scholar] reminded his contemporaries that in ancient times there had been no so-called "primary school." Small children had learned the rites from their fathers and seniors: they had first been taught filial piety, humility, self-discipline, and trustworthiness; the learning of texts came afterwards. Lung-ch'i (1630–93, native of P'ing-hu, Chekiang), the famous scholar-official, advised his son of the correct way to read the *Tso chuan* (Tso commentary on the *Spring and Autumn Annals*): "There are two kinds of characters (in the *Tso chuan*): the good and the bad. When you read the book you have to distinguish between the two. When you come across a good character, a feeling of admiration should be roused inside you [and you say to yourself,] 'I must desire to imitate him'; when you come across a bad character, a feeling of hatred should be roused inside you [and you say to yourself,] 'I must not imitate him'." For Liu Tsung-chou, the last session of the school day was to be consecrated to moral teaching: the teacher was to narrate and explain two stories that extolled loyalty, filial piety, and diligence. Pupils were to be constantly interrogated on the meaning of these stories so that they would not be lost from memory. Lü Te-sheng (d.1568), the father of Lü K'un, wrote a primer in rhyme entitled *Hsiao-erh yü* (Words of the child) incorporating most of these values and conveying a popularized version of the Chinese philosophy of life. His book became one of [the] most popular texts used in primary schools from the late Ming [seventeenth century] onward. . . .

Discipline

One can in general divide discipline in Ming-Ch'ing elementary schools into three categories: physical, social, and intellectual. Physical discipline was mainly to train the child's sense of cleanliness and orderliness and to exercise his body. According to classical Confucian training, each pupil had to take a turn sweeping the floor, cleaning the desks and the chairs of the classroom, and putting everything in order. Each also had to see to it that his attire was clean and his hair properly done. Lu Shih-i [scholar] tells us that by his time, that is the late seventeenth century, cleaning and sweeping of the home and of the classroom were almost exclusively done by servants. Very few stuck to the old training. For many educators, however, the daily cleaning of the classroom was in fact an excellent physical exercise for the pupils. Cleaning and sweeping were likely practiced symbolically as a kind of physical training. Social discipline was one of the most important aspects of elementary school education. The child was taught how to address his teacher and his classmates who were older or younger than he was as well as how and when to bow, walk, stand, sit, and take a meal properly. In other words, such discipline was to give him an elementary idea of his social position and the basic and formal rules of daily social intercourse with his superiors and inferiors.

Intellectual discipline was not as harsh as one might think. There were certainly strict and horrifying elementary schoolteachers, but they were certainly not the commonly accepted type of the time, at least not by the more enlightened educators. These latter authorities never harshly punished a child at the tender age of six or seven. Harsher punishments including standing, kneeling, and beating could only be used on children above eight or nine when words seemed to have no effect. Beating, which was divided into light and heavier degrees, was rarely to be employed (once every two to six months) so that children remained sensitive to it. Punishments were balanced against the system of rewards: paper, brushes, paper fans, and so on were given to worthy pupils. Punishment and rewards were only small parts of the methods used to discipline the child. For most educators, the essential thing was to keep the pupils intellectually occupied all the time [according to seventeenth-century educator Hsueh-ku, the purpose was] "to tighten their loosened hearts," "to tame and moderate their energy, and to prevent leisure [from getting into] their hearts." This training was to be practiced incessantly day after day with infinite patience by a teacher who was to display a serious expression at all times. After all, it was emphasized, since the great majority of pupils in elementary school would not sit for the imperial examination, the goal of elementary education was not to turn pupils into scholars within a short time but to tame them gradually into obedient and disciplined social beings.

The Yellow Emperor's Classic of Internal Medicine

Translated by Ilza Veith

Though Chinese legends suggest that *The Yellow Emperor's Classic of Internal Medicine* was written by the Yellow Emperor in the third millennium B.C., historians say it was put into its final form by scholars during the Han dynasty in around 206 B.C. As the classic text for Chinese medicine, the guide described diseases of the human body using the theory of the imbalance of yin (female, dark, passive) and yang (male, bright, assertive) energies. Physicians detected which force was dominant by examining a patient's pulse, and then prescribed treatment that could include acupuncture or Chinese herbs. Medical practitioners believed their job was to detect any yin-yang imbalance at an early stage and restore the harmony in the body before it manifested itself in illness. In the following extract, the Yellow Emperor says that the yin and yang principles are at the basis of all of creation and that their imbalance may lead to disharmony of the body or spirit.

In 1947 German-born Ilza Veith was the first person in the United States to be awarded a doctorate in the history of medicine. After graduating from Johns Hopkins University, she went on to become the vice chair of the department of history of health sciences at the University of California, specializing in the history of psychiatry and Far Eastern medicine.

The Yellow Emperor said: "The principle of Yin and Yang is the foundation of the entire universe. It underlies everything in creation. It brings about the development of parenthood; it is the root and source of life and death; it is found within the temples of the gods. In order to treat and cure diseases one must search for their origins.

"Heaven was created by the concentration of Yang, the force of light; Earth was created by the concentration of Yin, the force

The Yellow Emperor's Classic of Internal Medicine, translated by Ilza Veith. Baltimore, 1949.

of darkness. Yang stands for peace and serenity; Yin stands for confusion and turmoil. Yang stands for destruction; Yin stands for conservation. Yang brings about disintegration; Yin gives shape to things. . . .

"The pure and lucid element of light is manifested in the upper orifices, and the turbid element of darkness is manifested in the lower orifices. Yang, the element of light, originates in the pores. Yin, the element of darkness, moves within the five viscera [internal organs]. Yang, the lucid force of light, truly is represented by the four extremities; and Yin, the turbid force of darkness, stores the power of the six treasures of nature. Water is an embodiment of Yin, as fire is an embodiment of Yang. Yang creates the air, while Yin creates the senses, which belong to the physical body. When the physical body dies, the spirit is restored to the air, its natural environment. The spirit receives its nourishment through the air, and the body receives its nourishment through the senses. . . .

Imbalance of Yin and Yang

"If Yang is overly powerful, then Yin may be too weak. If Yin is particularly strong, then Yang is apt to be defective. If the male force is overwhelming, then there will be excessive heat. If the female force is overwhelming, then there will be excessive cold. Exposure to repeated and severe cold will lead to fever. Exposure to repeated and severe heat will induce chills. Cold injures the body while heat injures the spirit. When the spirit is hurt, severe pain will ensue. When the body is hurt, there will be swelling. Thus, when severe pain occurs first and swelling comes on later, one may infer that a disharmony in the spirit has done harm to the body. Likewise, when swelling appears first and severe pain is felt later on, one can say that a dysfunction in the body has injured the spirit. . . .

"Nature has four seasons and five elements. To grant long life, these seasons and elements must store up the power of creation in cold, heat, dryness, moisture, and wind. Man has five viscera in which these five climates are transformed into joy, anger, sympathy, grief, and fear. The emotions of joy and anger are injurious to the spirit just as cold and heat are injurious to the body. Violent anger depletes Yin; violent joy depletes Yang. When rebellious emotions rise to Heaven, the pulse expires and leaves the body. When joy and anger are without moderation, then cold and heat exceed all measure, and life is no longer secure. Yin and Yang should be respected to an equal extent.". . .

The Yellow Emperor asked, "Is there any alternative to the law of Yin and Yang?"

Ch'i Po [the Yellow Emperor's minister] answered: "When Yang is the stronger, the body is hot, the pores are closed, and people begin to pant; they become boisterous and coarse and do not perspire. They become feverish, their mouths are dry and sore, their stomachs feel tight, and they die of constipation. When Yang is the stronger, people can endure winter but not summer. When Yin is the stronger, the body is cold and covered with perspiration. People realize they are ill; they tremble and feel chilly. When they feel chilled, their spirits become rebellious. Their stomachs can no longer digest food and they die. When Yin is the stronger, people can endure summer but not winter. Thus Yin and Yang alternate. Their ebbs and surges vary, and so does the character of their diseases."

Harmonizing Yin and Yang

The Yellow Emperor asked, "Can anything be done to harmonize and adjust these two principles of nature?"

Ch'i Po answered: "If one has the ability to know the seven injuries and the eight advantages [Chinese treatments including acupuncture and use of medicinal herbs], one can bring the two principles into harmony. If one does not know how to use this knowledge, his life will be doomed to early decay. By the age of forty the Yin force in the body has been reduced to one-half of its natural vigor, and an individual's youthful prowess has deteriorated. By the age of fifty the body has grown heavy. The ears no longer hear well. The eyes no longer see clearly. By the age of sixty the life-producing power of Yin has declined to a very low level. Impotence sets in. The nine orifices no longer benefit each other. . . .

"Those who seek wisdom beyond the natural limits will retain good hearing and clear vision. Their bodies will remain light and strong. Although they grow old in years, they will stay able-bodied and vigorous and be capable of governing to great advantage. For this reason the ancient sages did not rush into the affairs of the world. In their pleasures and joys they were dignified and tranquil. They did what they thought best and did not bend their will or ambition to the achievement of empty ends. Thus their allotted span of life was without limit, like that of Heaven and Earth. This is the way the ancient sages controlled and conducted themselves. . . .

"By observing myself I learn about others, and their diseases become apparent to me. By observing the external symptoms, I gather knowledge about the internal diseases. One should watch for things out of the ordinary. One should observe minute and trifling things and treat them as if they were big and important. When they are treated, the danger they pose will be dissipated. Experts in examining patients judge their general appearance; they feel their pulse and determine whether it is Yin or Yang that causes the disease. . . . To determine whether Yin or Yang predominates, one must be able to distinguish a light pulse of low tension from a hard, pounding one. With a disease of Yang, Yin predominates. With a disease of Yin, Yang predominates. When one is filled with vigor and strength, Yin and Yang are in proper harmony."

Religions
and Rituals

CHAPTER

2

Chapter Preface

"Look at nothing contrary to ritual, hear nothing contrary to ritual, speak nothing contrary to ritual, do nothing contrary to ritual," said the sixth-century B.C. sage Kong Qiu, later known as Confucius, the founder of Confucianism, the major spiritual tradition of imperial China. Confucius believed that the correct observation of rituals was the key to promoting moral transformation of the individual, harmony within society, and order in the universe. He called for the re-creation of a formerly virtuous society by reviving ancient ritual practices known as *li*.

Drawing on ancient classical texts, Confucian scholars described the detailed requirements for *li*. Many of the important rituals observed by the Chinese paid homage to deceased ancestors. Confucian scholars stipulated the number of generations of ancestors that should be honored with sacrifices, and how elaborate the offerings should be for each level of society. Social status was the determining factor. Farmers, for example, were instructed to pay tribute to one or two past generations of ancestors with simple, private ceremonies offering fish and rice. Emperors, on the other hand, honored up to seven generations of ancestors in spectacular public ceremonies, sometimes including human sacrifices. In *Daily Life in China on the Eve of the Mongol Invasion, 1250–1276*, historian Jacques Gernet describes the ancestral rituals of the emperor in eleventh-century imperial China:

> A large temporary building was erected in front of the Supreme Temple in which to place the ceremonial chariot of the emperor. . . . Three days before [the ceremony], the Emperor . . . [purified] himself by fasting. . . . For this he donned the "hat of communication with Heaven," a tunic of fine silk, and various pendants. . . . [On the day of the ceremony] at the fourth beat of the drum, just before dawn, he donned his ceremonial headgear and went to sacrifice to his ancestors. During the night soldiers provided with torches and bearing the imperial insignia were posted on both sides of the great avenue. . . . When the Emperor mounted his chariot, all lights except those lining the route were extinguished. The imperial procession, led by tame elephants, now came through the processional gate. . . . The earth shook with the beat of drums and the solemn sound of trumpets. . . . The Em-

peror mounted the altar steps, which were covered with yellow gauze (the color of sovereignty). . . . A victim was sacrificed . . . and the Emperor offered libations to Heaven, to the August Earth and finally to his ancestors [to whom] he presented jade tablets along with ritual wine.

Not only did the Chinese honor their deceased ancestors through rituals, but they also paid tribute to other kinds of spirits. The villagers in rural China celebrated festivals to seek the blessing of deceased distinguished officials or ward off the evil spirits of departed souls who had been abandoned by their descendants. For example, in the Refining Fire Exorcism ritual celebrated in Shenzi village in southern China, villagers sought both the blessing of the departed spirit of Duke Hu, a powerful Chinese official of the tenth-century Song dynasty, and the exorcism of evil spirits that could sabotage their prosperity. During the ceremony, male villagers led by the local shaman, or spirit medium, walked across circular beds of red-hot charcoal. To the frantic beat of gongs and drums, the men whipped themselves into a frenzy before crossing the hot coals. As they became more and more agitated, the shaman filled his mouth with water from the offering table and sprayed the men three times in order to imbue them with the spirits of the dead. Just prior to their walking across the charcoal beds, the shaman, acting as the medium for Duke Hu's spirit, would declare:

I bless the entire village so that . . . domestic animals flourish, the . . . grains are harvested in abundance, the winds are mild and the rains seasonable, the country prosperous and the people at peace. I assist the yeoman tillers [farmers] so that when they till the fields, the fields produce grain. . . . I assist the merchant gentlemen so that one coin in capital yields ten thousand in interest. I assist the gentlemen in their prime . . . so that they might be as strong as dragons and tigers. I assist the elderly so that with ruddy complexions and white hair, they . . . return to youth. . . . I assist young maidens so that they may be clever and bright, like peach blossoms in a painting.

The Chinese believed that if they carefully observed such rituals, the souls of the departed would protect them from natural catastrophes and ensure good fortune for the family, the village, and the society. In their minds, the fate of the worlds of the living and the dead were interdependent, and both were linked to the preservation of order in the cosmos. "That the seas might take the place of the mountains, that the seasons might not follow their natural sequence, that Heaven and Earth might be confounded," writes Jacques Gernet, "these were the kind of . . . happenings that the ceremonies [honoring the departed] . . . were designed to avert." The energy and enthusiasm with which many contemporary Chinese continue to celebrate colorful and vibrant ceremonies throughout the year suggest that they still believe that human conduct affects order and harmony in the universe.

The Major Religious and Philosophical Ideas in Imperial China

Derk Bodde

Chinese religious and philosophical beliefs during the imperial age were based on a melding of Confucianism, Taoism, and Buddhism. In the following extract, Derk Bodde describes these traditional Chinese beliefs and how they differ from those held in the West and in other Eastern countries. Traditional Chinese culture was based on a code of ethics for interpersonal relations rather than on an organized religion. The Chinese perceived the universe in terms of the harmony between the interdependent forces of yin (feminine energy) and yang (masculine energy) rather than the conflict between good and evil. They also focused on the worlds of nature and humankind rather than on the supernatural realm. Derk Bodde is a professor emeritus of Chinese studies at the University of Pennsylvania. His published works include *A Short History of Chinese Philosophy* (1966) and *Chinese Thought, Society, and Science: The Intellectual and Social Background of Science and Technology in Pre-Modern China* (1991).

As a convenient method of procedure I propose to treat our subject under three heads: (1) the basic concepts of the Chinese as regards the world of the supernatural; (2) as regards the world of nature; and (3) as regards the world of man. In other words, what has been the prevailing Chinese attitude toward religion, toward the physical universe, and toward themselves? Adoption of such a division will give us a convenient framework within which to move, even though we must recognize that some ideas cannot be readily confined to any one of these three

Derk Bodde, "Dominant Ideas in the Formation of Chinese Culture," *Journal of the American Oriental Society*, vol. 62, December 1942.

categories, while others may conceivably escape the bounds of all of them together.

The World of the Supernatural

The first observation to be made here is a negative one. It is that the Chinese, generally speaking, have been less concerned with this world than with the other worlds of nature and of man. They are not a people for whom religious ideas and activities constitute an all important and absorbing part of life; and this despite the fact that there are, nominally, more Buddhists in China to-day than in any other country of the world. The significant point, in this connection, is that Buddhism came to China from the outside, and that before its impact in the first century A.D., China itself produced no thinker, with the doubtful exception of the philosopher, Mo Tzŭ (ca. 479–ca. 381 B.C.), who could be classed as a religious leader. It is ethics (especially Confucian ethics), and not religion (at least, not religion of a formal organized type), that has provided the spiritual basis of Chinese civilization.

The prevailing attitude of sophisticated Chinese toward the supernatural is perhaps best summed up by Confucius himself (551–479 B.C.), who once when asked by a disciple about the meaning of death, replied: "Not yet understanding life, how can you understand death?" Later thinkers have generally tended to adopt a skeptical attitude toward the unknown, and most of them, when they have ventured to express themselves on the subject have even gone to pains to deny that there can be such a thing as a personal immortality. All of which, of course, marks a difference of fundamental importance between China and most other major civilizations, in which a church and a priesthood have played a dominant role.

The preceding remarks do not mean, of course, that before the coming of Buddhism there were no religious manifestations in ancient China. What is important, however, is the fact that, from the very beginnings of Chinese history, the most vital and sincere form of religious feeling has been expressed in the worship of departed ancestors. And this has been of decisive importance, for ancestor worship, through its very nature, was a form of religion that could appeal to and be performed by only the immediate individual family groups concerned. Therefore it could not develop into a national or international organized faith similar to Christianity or other world religions.

Side by side with this ancestral cult, to be sure, various objects and forces of nature were also worshipped, such as sacred mountains, rivers, and the life-giving soil. These, however, were generally conceived of in abstract rather than personified terms, and even the supreme Chinese divinity, *T'ien* or Heaven, very rapidly lost its anthropomorphic qualities and became for most people a purely abstract ethical power. There was, therefore, no elaborate pantheon or mythology in ancient China. Likewise, there was no priesthood, because the worship of these divine forces was performed, not by the common people or by a priestly class, but almost entirely by the ruler himself, who, as the "Son of Heaven," acted as a sort of intermediary between the world of the supernatural and the world of man. Thus a pantheon, a mythology, or a priesthood are all comparatively late phenomena in China, connected either with Buddhism, or with the religious and popularized form of Taoism which developed, in part, as a Chinese imitation of the formal aspects of Buddhism.

It is true that the innumerable divinities of Buddhism and Taoism have in later times found a ready welcome among the Chinese masses, but this testifies more to the highly eclectic nature of the Chinese mind than to any strongly religious feeling. Because of this eclecticism the Chinese have, like the Hindus, for the most part been remarkably free from religious bigotry. The few persecutions that have occurred have usually been directed, not against religious ideas, but against religion as a social and political institution that might threaten the security of the secular state.

Finally, another fundamental difference between China and the civilizations of the Near East and of India, is the fact that in early China there was no idea of any kind of divine retribution after death. The whole concept of a system of rewards and punishments, meted out in a heaven or hell during a life hereafter, is utterly alien to Chinese thought and appears in China only with Buddhism.

The World of Nature

If the supernatural world has held a lesser place in China than in most other civilizations, quite the reverse is true of the second

of our three categories, the world of nature. For the Chinese, this
world of nature, with its mountains, its forests, its storms, its

Excerpts from the *Tao-te Ching*

*While Confucianism was the dominant creed during China's imperial age,
Taoism, a faith based on living simply and being at one with nature, ex-
erted a powerful influence on Chinese thinking. Historians say that its
main text, the* Tao-te Ching *("Classic of the Way and of Virtue"), was
written in the sixth century* B.C. *by an ascetic from south-central China
known as Lao-tzu. Below are three of the most famous passages of the
eighty-one verse text.*

Tao is empty (like a bowl).
It may be used but its capacity is never exhausted.
It is bottomless, perhaps the ancestor of all things.
It blunts its sharpness,
It unties its tangles.
It softens its light.
It becomes one with the dusty world.
Deep and still, it appears to exist forever.
I do not know whose son it is.
It seems to have existed before the Lord. . . .
The best (man) is like water.
Water is good; it benefits all things and does not compete with
    them.
It dwells in (lowly) places that all disdain.
This is why it is so near to Tao.
(The best man) in his dwelling loves the earth.
In his heart, he loves what is profound.
In his associations, he loves humanity.
In his words, he loves faithfulness.
In government, he loves order.
In handling affairs, he loves competence.
In his activities, he loves timeliness.
It is because he does not compete that he is without reproach. . . .
The softest things in the world overcome the hardest things in the
    world.
Non-being penetrates that in which there is no space.
Through this I know the advantage of taking no action.
Few in the world can understand the teaching without words and
    the advantage of taking no action.

Quoted in William Theodore de Bary and Richard Lufrano, eds., *Sources of Chinese
Tradition.* Vol. 2. New York: Columbia University Press, 1999.

mists, has been no mere picturesque backdrop against which to stage human events. On the contrary, the world of man and the world of nature constitute one great indivisible unity. Man is not the supremely important creature he seems to us in the western world; he is but a part, though a vital part, of the universe as a whole. This feeling conceivably may have originally sprung out of the overwhelmingly agrarian nature of Chinese civilization, and its consequent utter dependence, for survival itself, upon the continued regular succession of the forces of nature. Be that as it may, it is a feeling which has come to permeate a very large part of Chinese philosophy, art and literature.

In Taoism, the philosophy which has best expressed this mystic awareness of the oneness of the universe, we find many striking anticipations of the ideas that were propounded in the West by [eighteenth-century French philosopher Jean Jacques] Rousseau some two thousand years later. Like Rousseau, the Chinese Taoists said that human moral standards are artificial and hence invalid; that the appurtenances of civilization are corrupting; and that therefore we must cast off these man-made trammels and return to the state of nature. . . . Taoism also did away with human moral standards, but replaced them by a higher standard, that of the *Tao* or Way, the first cosmic principle of the universe which gives the Taoist school its name. Man, said the Taoists, must subordinate himself to the *Tao*, that is, to nature. This is not to be done by a facile giving in to one's emotions, but by a process of self discipline (through meditation and other means) that will result in a lessening of the desires and a consequent feeling of calm content amidst the simplicities of the natural life. In the final stage the Taoist devotee aims at entering a state of union with the surrounding universe, in which he is so completely freed from the bonds of human emotions that neither joy nor sorrow, life nor death, longer affect him. In this respect, Taoism remains in accord with the general stream of oriental mysticism.

This Taoist subordination of the self to the universe also differs importantly from another current of modern occidental thought. In the West happiness is to be found by harnessing the forces of nature to the will of man and thus increasing the means for man's material enjoyment. In China, on the contrary, the sage traditionally has been one who accords himself to the universe as he finds it, and thus gains what he considers to be the true happiness of contentment in simplicity. This concept, widely accepted in China, goes far to explain why Chinese, both educated and illiterate, can remain cheerful and even happy under poverty and primitive conditions that to a westerner would be intolerable. It has also been an important reason why the Chinese, though they developed remarkably scientific techniques in the compilation of their dictionaries, histories, encyclopaedias, and other scholarly works, failed to apply these techniques to the world of nature, and so failed to create a physical science.

Yin and Yang

Yet this prevailing attitude toward the physical universe—an attitude perhaps best summed up in [English poet William] Wordsworth's phrase as a "wise passiveness"—has not prevented the Chinese from attempting to classify and systematize the natural phenomena which they observed. In simplest terms, the Chinese theory of cosmogony [creation] (expressed, of course, with infinite variations by different writers) may be summarized as follows:

Lying behind the physical universe as we see it there exists an impersonal first cause or prime mover, known as the *Tao* or Way, from which all being has been evolved. This *Tao* manifests itself in the form of two all-inclusive principles: the *yang*, which is the principle of activity, heat, light, dryness, hardness, masculinity; and the *yin*, which is the principle of quiescence, cold, darkness, humidity, softness, femininity. Through the eternal interplay and interaction of these two principles, the five primary elements come into existence, these being fire (which is the essence of *yang*), water (which is the essence of *yin*), and earth, wood, and metal (which are combinations in varying degrees of the *yang* and the *yin*). These elements in their turn combine and recombine to produce all things in the universe, including Heaven (the sky, atmosphere, stars, etc.), which is preponderantly *yang*, and the Earth (the soil, plants, animals, etc.), which is preponderantly *yin*. Everything in the universe thus pertains to one or another of the five elements, and the Chinese have compiled long lists of categories in fives, such as the five colors, five smells, five tastes, five tones, five internal organs, etc., with which to correlate the five elements.

This splitting up of the world into sets of fives is a typical manifestation of the rationalistic Chinese mind, which tries to find order and plan in all things, and which has therefore taken a particular delight in inventing numerical categories of all kinds, not only in fives, but in many other numbers. The theory of the *yin* and *yang*, the five elements, and their correlates, has for more than two thousand years been the basis for Chinese medicine, alchemy, astronomy, and naturalistic speculation generally. . . .

In connection with this theory of cosmogony, it is important that we should distinguish clearly between the Chinese dualistic system based upon the interplay of the *yin* and *yang* principles, and the superficially similar dualisms of light and darkness, good and evil, etc., with which we are familiar in the Near East and in the occidental world. The latter dualisms are all based upon the concept of mutual antagonism between their two conflicting members; of the goodness of the one and the evilness of the other; and of the consequent necessity to conquer the evil so that the good may eventually triumph. They are often closely connected with religion.

The *yin-yang* dualism, on the contrary, is based, not upon mutual opposition, but upon mutual harmony. The feminine *yin* and the masculine *yang* are equally essential if there is to exist a universe. Each is complementary to the other, and neither is necessarily superior or inferior from a moral point of view. In this concept we see a striking manifestation of the Chinese tendency . . . to find in all things an underlying harmony and unity, rather than struggle and chaos. In it, the Chinese would seem to have come closer to the ideas lying behind much of modern science, than have we in the West with our traditional good-versus-evil type of dualism.

The World of Man

When we turn to the third of our three categories, that of the world of man, we find ourselves at the heart of the greater part of Chinese philosophical speculation. How to get along equably with one's fellow men: this is the problem that Confucianism set itself to answer, just as Taoism posed for itself the problem of how man can adjust himself to the outer universe. The Chinese, with sound common sense, have from very early times realized that unless there can be a solution to this central problem of human relationship, material power and progress will but serve to increase the afflictions of mankind. Being a practical, realistic, and pragmatic people, they launched their frontal attack upon this vital question, and in so doing have produced a great mass of ethical and political philosophy. . . .

Coupled with this intense preoccupation with human affairs is the Chinese feeling for *time*; the feeling that human affairs should be fitted somehow into a temporal framework. The result has been the accumulation of a tremendous and unbroken body of historical literature, extending over more than three thousand years, such as is unequalled by any other people. This history has served in China a distinctly moral purpose, for by studying the past one might learn how to conduct oneself in the present and future. Hence the writing of history was commonly not left merely to the whim of a few historically minded individuals. Ever since the founding of the first long lived empire in the second century B.C., one of the first duties of a conquering dynasty has been to compile the history of the dynasty it supplanted, often appointing for that purpose a large board of government-supported scholars, who were set to work upon the historical archives of the preceding dynasty. The resulting dynastic histories were not limited to a bald narration of political events. They included also valuable essays on such subjects as economics, law, water-control works, astronomy, bibliography, geography, and many other topics, as well as the biographies of hundreds of illustrious individuals. . . .

What was the nature of the society that the Chinese thus took such pains to record? It was not one that believed in what we would call rugged individualism. Rather, Confucianism aimed at teaching each individual how to take his place with the least possible friction in his own social group, and how to perform his allotted duties within that group in such a way as would bring the greatest benefit to the group as a whole. The basic and most important unit of Chinese society was the family or clan, to which the individual owed his first allegiance, and which he served, first by sacrificing to the ancestors who were dead; secondly, by caring for the elder generation who were still living; and thirdly, by rearing descendants of his own who would carry on the family line. In return, the family acted as a protective group of mutual aid, shielding the individual from an often hostile outer world. Through its cohesiveness, it succeeded in maintaining the fabric of Chinese life and culture even in times of almost complete social and political collapse. Because of this stress upon family in China, there has been a correspondingly limited development of nationalistic feeling (save in a vague cultural sense), and little of that fiery patriotism so exalted in the West.

Obligations of Ruler and Ruled

Beyond the family, nevertheless, lay the state, which was regarded simply as an enlargement of the family unit. Thus even to-day the term for "nation" in Chinese, literally translated, means "national family," while it was common in the past for the emperor to refer to himself as "the parent of the people." In this society each individual occupied a definite position and was held accordingly responsible for the performance of stated duties. Yet paternalistic though it was, the system certainly did not (in theory, at least) operate solely for the benefit of a ruling class. If inferiors were expected to serve their superiors with loyalty, superiors were equally bound by certain definite obligations toward their inferiors. Confucianism stressed the reciprocal nature of these duties and obligations. It also emphasized that the primary duty of the ruler is to give good government to his people, and that to do this he must himself set a high moral standard and select with care the officials who serve under him. It thus attached great importance to the power of personal example of men in public life, and the need for their moral self cultivation.

Owing to the development of a very intensive agricultural economy, stimulated in part, at least, by a widespread government-fostered system of irrigation works, it was possible in China for a large population to subsist upon a comparatively small amount of land. Having this large population, the Chinese empire spread to huge proportions and developed into an exceedingly complex bureaucracy, employing a vast army of officials. Yet despite its size and all inclusive character, the Chinese state remained sufficiently fluid and flexible to leave a place for considerable social change and individual initiative. It aimed at moral suasion rather than legalistic compulsion, and definitely rejected the somewhat cold and mechanical approach to government, based on law, which has been such a cornerstone of occidental civilization. Law codes, of course, existed, but they were subject to a considerable degree of individual judgment and interpretation, which was based upon the handed-down body of traditional experience and morality known as *li*.

Social Mobility

It was quite possible, therefore, in Chinese society, especially in times of political change, for determined individuals to work their way up to high positions, a feat accomplished several times in history by founders of dynasties who rose from quite humble origins. Women, similarly, though before the law they held an inferior position, yet in point of fact quite frequently exercised very considerable power within their family group. Thus China has produced a goodly number, not only of famous beauties, but also of female painters, poets, historians, and empresses. There was, in fact, little in Chinese society suggestive of any hard and fixed stratification into unchanging social groups.

The moral basis for this society was the belief, shared by the majority of Chinese thinkers, that man is by nature fundamentally good; that there is no such thing as original sin; and that therefore any person, even the lowliest, is potentially capable of becoming a sage. Evil, according to the Chinese view, does not exist as a positive force in itself; it is simply the result of a temporary deflection from the essential harmony of the universe. With these concepts go the optimism, the good humor, and the wil to live, that are marked characteristics of so many Chinese. The Indian dictum that life is suffering was inconceivable to the Chinese mind and even with the coming of Buddhism never succeeded in gaining general acceptance.

Because they believed that all men can be taught morality, the Chinese attached an importance hardly paralleled elsewhere upon the value of learning. "Wisdom" was included by them among the five cardinal virtues, meaning by this an understanding of right and wrong and of moral principles generally. Hence the Chinese stress upon their classics, which they regarded as containing deep moral truths; upon history as an instrument whereby man may be taught to avoid the mistakes of his forefathers; and eventually upon all humanistic scholarship.

All this led to the creation of what has been the most distinctive feature of Chinese government, the famed examination system. Other countries have until recent times with few exceptions been ruled by a hereditary aristocracy, a priesthood, a military hierarchy, or a rich merchant class. But in China, ever since the creation of the first long lived empire in the second century B.C., entry into the bureaucracy that governed the country was limited to those who succeeded in passing a series of very strict governmental examinations, based upon a thorough knowledge of the Chinese classics. Service in this official bureaucracy was the highest goal which one could attain, and therefore success in the examinations was the highest aim.

Such, at least, was the theory. In practice, the system naturally operated best in periods of strong political unity, while in times of strife or dynastic change it tended to break down. Likewise, it contained certain manifest defects, such as its undue stress upon memory, and the fact that the wealthy naturally enjoyed superior opportunities to acquire the education that would make success possible.

Nevertheless, when all is said and done, the fact remains that the examinations provided an impartial and purely intellectual test that had to be surmounted by each and every individual through his own efforts alone if he were to enter the coveted ranks of the scholar-officials. Likewise, the examinations were open to all members of society alike, with but trifling exceptions. . . .

Unity and Harmony

Before closing . . . I should like to reaffirm the importance of one concept to which I have already more than once alluded, namely, the fundamental oneness and harmony of the Chinese *Weltanschauung* [philosophy of life]. In the Chinese mind, there is no real distinction between the world of the supernatural, the world of nature, and the world of man. They are all bound up in one all-embracing unity. "All things are complete with me," proclaims the Confucian, Mencius (371?–279? B.C.), thus echoing the sentiment of the Taoist, Chuang Tzŭ (ca. 369–ca. 286 B.C.) who says: "Heaven and Earth came into being with me together, and with me, all things are one."

As applied to social relationships, these concepts manifest themselves in the emphasis of Chinese writers upon restraint, tolerance, equanimity, and pursuit of the golden mean. "Let the states of equilibrium and harmony exist in perfection, and a happy order will prevail throughout Heaven and Earth, while all things will be nourished and prosper." So says the *Doctrine of the Mean* [Confucian moral text], one of the works that was formerly learned by heart in the traditional system of education.

Confucian Teachings

Confucius

The Chinese sage Confucius (551–479 B.C.), known as K'ung Ch'iu to his disciples, was the founder of Confucianism, an ethical code that formed the spiritual basis of imperial society. The *Analects of Confucius* (derived from *analekta*, the Greek word for "selection") is considered the most important written source of his thought. The work consists of a selection of conversations between the Chinese sage and his disciples, which was recorded by his later followers. In the following extract, Confucius says that devotion to the family, consideration of others, and the faithful conduct of ritual obligations are the basic requirements for social stability and good government.

Human Nature

The master said, "In terms of human nature, people are much alike. But in terms of practice and effort, they are quite different."

Confucius said, "Those who are possessed of understanding from birth are the highest type of people. Those who understand things only after studying them are of the next lower type, and those who learn things from painful experience are yet the next. Those who have painful experiences but do not learn from them are the lowest type of people."

The Honorable Person

The master said, "Isn't one truly an honorable person if one is not acknowledged by others yet still does not resent it!"

The master said, "Honorable people are modest in what they say but surpassing in what they do."

Heaven

The master said, "Honorable persons seek things within themselves. Small-minded people, on the other hand, seek things from others."

Confucius, "The Analects of Confucius," *Chinese Religion: An Anthology of Sources*, edited by Deborah Sommer. New York: Oxford University Press, 1995.

Confucius said, "There are three things of which the honorable person is in awe: the mandate of heaven, great people, and the words of the sages. Small-minded people do not understand the mandate of heaven and are not in awe of it; they are insolent toward great people and ridicule sages."

Humanity, Virtue, and Consideration

The master rarely spoke of profit, of one's mandated fate, or of humanity.

The master said, "Persons possessed of humanity are like this: wanting to develop themselves, they also develop others; wanting to achieve things themselves, they also allow others to achieve what they want. This is the direction humanity takes: to use what is close to oneself as an analogy to be extended to others."

Chung-kung [a disciple] asked about humanity. The master said, "In your social affairs behave as if you are meeting with important guests, and treat people as if you were participating in a great sacrificial offering. Do not impose on other people anything you yourself dislike. Let there be no animosity either in the state or in the family." Chung-kung said, "Even though I am not gifted, I will try to practice what you have just said."

Fan Ch'ih [a disciple] asked about humanity. The master said, "Be solicitous of others." Fan Ch'ih asked about understanding. The master said, "Be understanding toward others."

The master said, "Only persons possessed of humanity can truly like other people or truly dislike them."

The master said, "Is humanity something far away? If I want to be humane, then humanity has already been attained."

Someone asked. "What of repaying animosity with virtue?" The master said, "How could one repay that with virtue? Repay animosity with directness, and repay virtue with virtue."

Tzu-kung [a senior disciple] asked, "Is there one word by which one may live one's entire life?" The master said, "Isn't that word 'consideration'? Do not impose on other people anything you yourself dislike."

The Way

The master said, "It is enough that someone who dies in the evening has heard of the Way only that morning."

The master said, "Tseng-tzu, my way has only one theme that holds it all together." Tseng-tzu replied, "That is so." When the master went out, the other disciples asked Tseng-Tzu what Confucius had meant. Tseng-tzu replied, "The master's way is simply loyalty and consideration."

It is that human beings glorify the Way, not that the Way glorifies human beings.

Governance

The master said, "Someone who governs with virtue is like the northern polar star, which stays in one place while all the other stars pay their respects to it."

Chi-k'ang Tzu [a disciple] asked Confucius about governance. Confucius replied, "To govern means to rectify. If you start by rectifying yourself, how would anyone else not do the same?"

The master said, "If you rectify your own self, then even if you give no orders they will still be carried out. If you don't rectify yourself, then even if you do give orders they will still not be followed."

The master said, "If one adopts administrative measures and implements punishments in a consistent fashion, the people will comply with them but will have no shame. But if one follows the Way of virtue and implements ritual consistently, the people will have a sense of shame and moreover will correct themselves.". . .

Ritual

The master said, "People say 'ritual this' and 'ritual that.' But is ritual just jades and silks? They say 'music this' and 'music that.' But is music just bells and drums?"

[Disciple] Yen Yüan asked about humanity. The master said, "If one can prevail over the self and turn toward ritual, that is humanity. If one can do this for just a single day, the whole world will incline toward humanity. But is it that humanity just comes from one's own self alone, or from interacting with other people!" Yen Yüan said, "I would like to ask about the specific details of this." The master said, "Look at nothing contrary to ritual; hear nothing contrary to ritual, speak nothing contrary to ritual, do nothing contrary to ritual." Yen Yüan said, "Even though I am not gifted, I will try to practice what you have just said."

The Life of Confucius

In Sources of Chinese Tradition, *William Theodore de Bary and Richard Lufrano describe the life of Confucius, whose teachings shaped Chinese politics and culture throughout the imperial age.* Ru *was a term used by Confucius to refer to virtuous people who were committed to learning and right conduct rather than to military prowess.*

Early sources suggest that Confucius was born in the feudal state of Lu in eastern China into a family of the lower ranks of the nobility, one that was probably in straitened circumstances. It is clear that by the middle of the sixth century the Zhou dynasty, whose founders he honored, was in an advanced state of decline, having lost much of its real power and authority some two centuries earlier. Warfare was endemic, as the rulers of contending states vied for territory and power. Uncertainty surrounded the future of those states, and in the eyes of many, shrouded the fate of civilization itself. Confucius emerged as one of a number of scholars who responded to an apparent crisis of civilization. He traveled from one feudal state to another, seeking an audience with various rulers and hoping to be employed by one capable of sharing his vision. He put forward the perspective of the *ru*—his purpose having been to promote the style and manners of the noble person (*junzi*) and the efficacy of moral force or virtue (*de*), rather than violence and coercion, as a strategy for rulers. Toward the end of his life, disappointed but evidently unembittered by his failure to gain an influential political office, he continued in the role of a teacher to promote these same causes. Not immediately, but over a period of centuries, the significance of Confucius as a teacher would become apparent, and within a century or so he would acquire the reputation of a sage. In subsequent centuries his example would be woven into the fabric of an entire culture as perhaps its most persistent pattern.

William Theodore de Bary and Richard Lufrano, eds., *Sources of Chinese Tradition.* Vol. 2. New York: Columbia University Press, 1999.

The master said, "What does someone not possessed of humanity have to do with ritual? What does someone not possessed of humanity have to do with music?"

[Disciple] Lin Fang asked about the fundamental basis of ritual. The master replied, "That is a good question! In performing rituals it is better to be simple rather than extravagant. For rites of mourning it is better to be sorrowful rather than casual."

When Fan Ch'ih was Confucius's charioteer, the master said, "Meng-sun asked me what filiality was and I said, 'Not being disobedient.'" Fan Ch'ih asked, "What did you mean by that?" The master replied, "I meant to serve one's parents with ritual when they are alive, to bury them with ritual when they die, and thereafter to sacrifice to them with ritual."

Tzu-kung wanted to eliminate the offering of the sacrificial sheep at the beginning of the lunar month. The master said, "Tzu-kung, you are concerned about the sheep, but I am concerned about the ritual."

The master said, "Honorable people, widely studied in cultured things and guided by ritual will not overstep themselves."

The master said, "Respect without ritual becomes tiresome, circumspection without ritual becomes timidity, bold fortitude without ritual becomes unruly, and directness without ritual becomes twisted."

The Dragon Boat Race Festival

Yang Szu-ch'ang

Festivals played an important role in peoples' lives in imperial China. They reinforced ways of understanding the world, strengthened group identification, and gave people the opportunity to vent emotions that could not be expressed in everyday life. Their main purpose was to attract good luck and prosperity and to remove evil spirits.

On the fifth day of the fifth month, the Chinese celebrated the dragon boat race festival, when boatmen from adjacent towns would compete in a boat race in vessels that looked like dragons. In Chinese mythology, dragons controlled the waters and dispensed the rain, and the Chinese believed that the fierce competition of the race would stimulate real dragon fights in the heavens and ensure heavy rain for a good harvest. In preparation for the race, the people cast rice upon the waters to feed the souls of those who had drowned and set lanterns adrift to draw the hungry ghosts to the feast. Yang Szu-ch'ang (1588–1641), who lived in Hunan in northern China in the late Ming dynasty, wrote the following personal account of the dragon boat race festival.

T he dragon boat race originated in the old Yüan and Hsiang regions as a ceremony to call back Ch'ü Yüan.[1] Being north of the Tung-t'ing Lake, our Wu-ling is part of Yüan (Ch'ang-sha, south of the Lake, is in the old Hsiang) and therefore the boat race flourishes here. Since we inherited it directly from the state of Ch'u of the Chou dynasty [557–588] it is only natural that our boat race cannot be matched by that of any other province.

The boat race is held at the center of the prefectural seat [central area governed by a senior official or prefect]. The most dis-

---

1. Ch'ü Yüan was a fourth-century B.C. government minister who drowned himself after being discharged from his post by the king for his slanderous ways.

Yang Szu-ch'ang, "The Dragon Boat Race in Wu-Ling, Hunan," translated by Chao Wei-pang, *Folklore Studies 2*, 1943, pp. 1–18.

tant places from which boats still come are Yü-chia-kang, fifteen *li* [about 3 miles] downstream, and Pai-sha-tu, thirty-five *li* upstream. On the day of the festival, flagmen and drummers on boats going to and fro make a deafening noise heard for about fifty *li*. The race course runs for about ten *li* along the southern shore from Tuan-chia-tsui to Ch'ing-ts'aotsui and along the northern shore from Shang-shih-kuei. The river is wide there and well suited for a race course. The southern shore is covered with grass, forests, and snowy white sands. On the northern shore are high buildings with beautifully painted balconies and old city walls. The spectators gather there. . . .

The current popular belief is that the boat race is held to avert misfortunes. At the end of the race, the boats carry sacrificial animals, wine, and paper coins and row straight downstream, where the animals and wine are cast into the water, the paper coins are burned, and spells are recited. The purpose of these acts is to make pestilence and premature death flow away with the water. This is called "sending away the mark." Then the boats row back without flags and drumbeating. They will be pulled onto land and housed in huts on the shore till the next year, as this year's races are over. About this time the people have rites performed to ward off fires. Also, those who are ill make paper boats in the same color as the dragon boat of their region and burn them at the shore. . . .

Role of the Shaman

Shamans [spirit mediums] are employed during the boat races in order to suppress evil influence. Sometimes people go to the mountains to invite famous shamans, called "mountain teachers," who are especially skillful. The night before the race, the headman provides sacrificial animals and wine and asks the shaman to perform. The shaman jumps head over heels from the bow to the stern. Buckwheat is scattered and a fire is lighted. This is called "brightening the boat." Drums are beaten throughout the night to ward off the influences of opposing shamans, who, if caught, might be beaten to death.

On the day of the races the shaman makes an oil fire to launch the boat. He can foresee unfailingly the victory or defeat of the boat from the color and height of the flame. The god he serves is called the Immortal of Hsi-ho-sa. The shaman's spells include "the furious fire of the violent thunder burning Heaven." His finger-charms include "arresting the front dragons," "stopping the devil-soldiers," and "moving the mountains and overturning the seas." With his trouser legs rolled up and his feet bare, he jumps seven steps and then throws water into the fire. When the fire rises again, the boat starts. Some sentences of his spell are: "The Heaven fire burns the sun. The Earth fire burns the five directions. The thunder fire, executing the law, burns to death the various inauspicious things. The dragon boat taking to the water will float at will in the five lakes and four seas." The outer side of the bottom of the boat is swept with a bundle of reeds from stem to stern in order to prevent anything from being hung on the boat by an enemy. The other ceremonies, being secret, cannot be described.

Patrons and Headmen

The man chosen as the headman of a racing boat must be brave and have a family. Several days before, he distributes steamed cakes and pieces of paper to those who belong to his region and is repaid in money. On the top of the pieces of paper pictures of dragon boats are printed and on the bottom some sentences are written.

Supplying food and wine during the race is assigned to rich men, who are honored if they contribute generously. Others supply food because they have made a vow to do so. On the day of the races there are small boats in the river bringing food. They are decorated with two trees of paper money and colored silks, and musicians play in them. The boatmen must force in the food and wine beyond the point of satiation until nothing is left. Otherwise anything left has to be thrown into the water together with the dishes and chopsticks.

In the evening when the boats return, the people take the water in the boats, mix it with various grasses, and use it to wash their bodies. This is said to prevent bad luck and is a kind of purification.

The boatmen are all familiar with the water and are expert swimmers, but the headman, flagman, drummer, and clapper need not be able to swim, as the oarsmen are responsible for their lives. On the day of the races all wear on their heads the charms furnished by the shaman and stick small reddish-yellow flags with egret feathers in the hair at their temples to ward off evil. The spectators display red or green pieces of silk, some with sentences written on them, and give them to the passing dragon boats as presents. As a boat passes by its home base, the people set off fireworks, wave their fans, and applaud. If the boat belongs to some other place, they shout ridicule at it, some of them getting angry and even throwing tiles at it. The boatmen respond by grabbing their oars or gesturing to show their willingness to fight. . . .

Fierce Competition

Each boat belongs to a distinct region, and the people of its home base quarrel with those of the others about who won and who lost. Even the children and women do not admit defeat. Most men who have moved away from where their ancestors lived are still loyal to the boat of their ancestral region. But others who have moved do not root for any boat, which makes them despised by their neighbors as cowardly. At this time, while playing chess, guessing fingers, and even when drinking people say nothing but "victory." Sometimes they shout "*tung, tung*" to imitate the sound of the drums; sometimes they wave their sleeves to accompany the rowing and cry "victory! victory!" It is the custom to have this kind of enthusiasm for the races. Officials, stationed within the territories of the different boats should not join the contending groups, but, in fact, they are also divided according to the popular way of thinking. . . .

The people watch the boat races from the shore. Along the northern shore from Ch'ing-p'ing-men to Shih-kuei, about five or six *li*, are buildings of three or four stories in which space can be reserved by paying an advance fee of up to several hundred cash. On the day of the races, the people, carrying wine bottles and food boxes, ride on carts and horses or walk along the roads to get there by mid-morning. Tables are covered with fruit and food for sale. The best fruits are the "plums from the Han family" and the "wheat-yellow peaches"; the food includes shad and vegetables. When the start of the race is announced, everyone stops talking, laughing, or leaning against the balustrades. Attentively they watch, wondering which is their boat and whether it will meet victory or defeat. All too quickly victory is decided. Then some are so proud it seems as if their spirits could break the ceiling, and some have faces pale as death and seem not to know how to go down the stairs. . . .

The people can only rent space in buildings within their respective regions. Those who belong to the flower or the white boat do not enter the region of the black boat; those of the black or the red boat do not enter that of the flower boat. No one would do so consciously unless he wanted a fight, because sometimes terrible consequences result.

Victors and Losers

Because there are too few buildings for all the spectators, there are numerous food shelters on the southern shore and house boats in the river. People on the southern shore can see quite clearly as the boats cross the river from the northern to the southern bank. When a boat nears a bank, if it does not belong to their region, people fling stones at it, and the men on the beat wave their oars menacingly. The spectators' boats in the river often obstruct the route of the racing boats. If a boat happens to be just in front of a racing boat and cannot get out of the way, it can be broken to pieces in seconds. . . .

The victorious boat rows with its stern forward. The men hold their oars vertically, dance, and beat gongs on the boat. When they pass a losing boat, they threaten it. Those losing try to do the same but with less spirit, or if a little further behind, they silently acknowledge defeat. At sunset the boats disperse. At the home of the headmen, feasts are prepared and the boatmen all gather to dine. At the victor's home, food and wine are especially abundant and his neighbors, relatives, and friends come to offer congratulations. The next day, the door of his house will be beautifully decorated with colored silk, and a feast and a dramatic performance will be held. Some people write sentences or short poems on the city gates to ridicule the losers, or tie up a dog or a tortoise with some grass and fruit and place them there for the same purpose. When the men of the defeated boats happen to pass by, they lower their heads and go on their way. Their relatives or friends sometimes send such things to them to make fun of them.

From the fourth month the people begin to talk enthusiastically about the boats. In the fifth month the race is held and victory and defeat are decided. Yet even by the eighth or ninth month the people are still not tired of the subject.

Working Life

CHAPTER
3

Chapter Preface

The working life of each social class in imperial society was guided by principles of moral conduct developed by the sixth-century B.C. sage Confucius. Founder of imperial China's main spiritual tradition, Confucianism, Confucius envisioned the ideal society as one based on moral order: Each person would act in accordance with specific codes of conduct for his or her position in society consistent with the virtues of duty, honesty, integrity, and consideration of others. Throughout the imperial age, Confucian scholars wrote detailed guides for the conduct of each occupational group based on these virtues.

Scholars instructed the members of the gentry class about their special responsibilities to educate the common people about Confucian values and to intervene if disputes arose. One set of regulations developed by a seventeenth-century Ming dynasty scholar instructed the gentry:

> Rectify your own conduct and transform the common people.
> If people have suffered injustice, expose it and correct it.
> Try to settle complaints and grievances among others.
> Protect virtuous people.
> Urge others to esteem charity and disdain personal gain.
> Influence others to cherish good deeds.

Confucian scholars also wrote guides instructing farmers and merchants to act in accordance with Confucian virtues. For example, farmers were instructed not to steal their masters' grain nor damage their neighbors' crops out of envy for their flourishing fields. Farmers were also guided to be diligent in their daily duties, to rise early to work, and to be considerate of the world of nature by refraining from harming animals when fertilizing their fields and from needlessly hurting insects.

Confucian scholars instructed merchants to be honest in their dealings with the people and to have compassion for the poor. As Confucius had said, "Wealth and high rank . . . attained unrighteously are to me but floating clouds." The scholars' guides also admonished merchants not to obtain fortunes by exploiting the people. As one guide written by a seventeenth-century Confucian scholar stated:

Do not deceive ignorant villagers when fixing the price of goods.
Do not use short measure when selling and long measure when
buying.
When a debtor owes you a small sum but is short of money, have
mercy and forget about the difference. Do not bring him bank-
ruptcy and hatred by refusing to come to terms.

Although Confucian scholars did not write guides for the
moral conduct of people in vocations outside the mainstream of
society, these groups had ways of defining and enforcing their
own ethical standards. For example, beggars in the urban centers belonged to guilds that set strict standards for their conduct.
Leaders of beggars in a specific geographic area told guild members whom they could approach and when. For example, they
instructed beggars not to bother families celebrating rituals once
those families had donated the appropriate amount to the head
beggar according to guild regulations. He would then distribute
the money to the beggars in that area and force those who did
not respect this etiquette to leave the area.

Similarly, although they had no Confucian scholars' texts to
consult, eunuchs, castrated males employed by the imperial
palace to protect the chastity of the women of the emperor's
harem, had an unwritten ethical code. This code demanded loyalty to the emperor and discretion concerning his affairs. Often,
however, eunuchs failed to live up to these principles, and eunuchs of the Han (206 B.C.–A.D. 220), Tang (619–906), and Ming
(1368–1644) dynasties became embroiled in palace intrigues.
These eunuchs reputedly contributed to the people's disillusion-
ment with the emperors and the downfall of the dynasties.

Although people did not always follow the rules for proper conduct, Confucian values effectively shaped society through the pro-
liferation of written and unwritten codes for the people in each
occupational group. Confucius believed that if people lived according to these guidelines, they would invite the blessings of
heaven, and if they failed to fulfill their obligations, they would
suffer serious consequences. "If one truly . . . fulfills the duties appropriate to his way of life; if one upholds public and private obligations . . . one invites Heaven's favor," wrote one seventeenth-
century Confucian scholar, "[for] Heaven responds to human vices
with punishments as surely as an echo follows a sound."

The Life of a Farmer

Michael Loewe

Agriculture formed the backbone of imperial China's economy and society. Extracting a living from the soil was considered the principal work of humanity, and the revenues of imperial governments rested on the prosperity reaped from the land. Accordingly, the farmer's occupation was honored and respected, and coordinated efforts of family members to ensure a good harvest were the focus of daily life for the majority of Chinese.

In the following selection from *Everyday Life in Early Imperial China During the Han Period*, Michael Loewe describes the annual activities, farming methods, and seasonal and family rituals practiced by farmers in early imperial China. Loewe was a lecturer in Chinese studies at Cambridge University from 1963 to 1990. He has also edited a number of books on life in ancient and early imperial China, including *Early Chinese Texts: A Bibliographical Guide* (1994) and *The Cambridge History of Ancient China: From the Origins of Civilization to 221 B.C.* (1999), which he edited with Edward L. Shaughnessy.

The farmers' main occupation lay in the production of life's necessities, i.e., grain for food, and hemp for the coarse raiment in which most of the population were clothed. But where land and climate permitted, the countryman could raise reasonably high profits by other undertakings; by stock-breeding or pasturing horses or cattle, sheep or pigs; by keeping fish-farms or maintaining timber-woods and bamboo-groves. Fruit-growing was practised in both the north and the south, as and where conditions favoured chestnut, date or citrus fruit. Some countrymen made a living from mulberry orchards and the product of the silkworm, or from the lac tree whose lacquer was used so lavishly for decorative purposes by the wealthy; and market-gardeners who lived near the cities could ply a trade in vegetables or seasonings such as leeks or ginger. As yet there was no widespread growth of tea, cotton or sugar. The tea-bush was doubtless known in

Michael Loewe, *Everyday Life in Early Imperial China During the Han Period, 202 B.C.–A.D. 220*. New York: Dorset Press, 1968. Copyright © 1968 by Michael Loewe. Reproduced by permission of the author.

some parts of the south, but the drink did not yet feature as a daily or common beverage. Knowledge of the grape had been brought from the trade-routes that led to Central Asia, and vineyards were kept for the use of the Palace. The spirits that were distilled somewhat extravagantly from grain made their appearance at religious functions and occasions of merry-making, and supplies were sometimes distributed by imperial bounty. Cane-sugar was probably grown in the south but some centuries had to pass before its distribution became general. Sheep were kept for mutton or for their fleeces which could be shaped into warm garments; but the Han [dynasty, 206 B.C.–A.D. 220] Chinese were not accustomed to process sheep's wool into textiles, as were their neighbours in Central Asia. . . .

Tools and Implements

A number of mechanical contrivances had been devised to aid the Han farmer in his work. Long hammers were laid out horizontally, with the central point resting on a fulcrum where it could pivot; and at the end opposite the head, a man would stand on pedals, speeding the machine into action. There must have been several uses for these hammers other than beating the husks off grain (e.g., pounding earth, in the processes of building); and there is some evidence to suggest that Han engineers had succeeded in harnessing animal-power and water-power to operate these hammers mechanically. Fans were used to separate the chaff from the kernels of the grain. These were fitted to containers into which the grain was fed, and a crank handle was sometimes used to turn the wheel. The final reduction of grain to flour was done first by means of pestles and mortars, some of which were made in bronze; but there were also handmills worked with a circular movement, and probably made of wood, baked clay or stone. It is also possible that towards the end of the Han period milling was done by means of a cylindrical roller drawn evenly across the grain.

Perhaps the most arduous, necessary and continuous task that faced the farmer was that of lifting water from the wells or irrigation channels to maintain a steady and constant supply to the fields. One of the simplest aids took the form of a pole suspended horizontally, to swing over a central vertical support. A bucket was attached to the end that lay immediately over the water, and

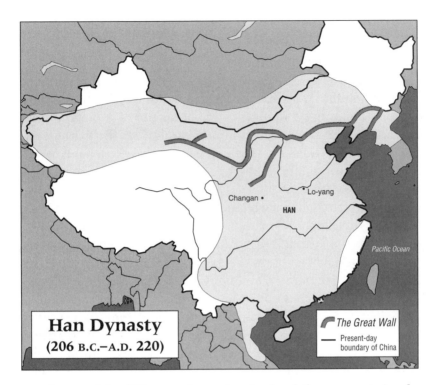

Changan •   • Lo-yang

HAN

Pacific Ocean

Han Dynasty
(206 B.C.–A.D. 220)

The Great Wall
— Present-day
boundary of China

was lowered for filling; and to raise the load the peasant simply fitted a counter-weight at the opposite end of the pole, thus lifting the bucket to the required level. From models that were buried in tombs we know that some wells were fitted with a protective housing and roof, and that a pulley was built-in, so that buckets could be raised or lowered by rope. The elevation of water from irrigation channels that lay below the level of the fields was probably done by human foot-power. By revolving a horizontal shaft to which an endless chain had been fitted, it was possible to depress a series of empty compartments or containers into the stream and bring them back filled, so that their contents could be delivered into the fields. At a later period this type of pumping device was operated by water-power or animal-power; and it has by no means been abandoned in the face of the more modern techniques of the twentieth century.

Ts'ui Shih's Rules for Husbandry

We possess no detailed contemporary record of the Han countryman's year whose value can compare with that of the manorial records or illuminated manuscripts which bear witness to the life of the farmer in mediaeval Europe. But fragments of a short text on husbandry that is ascribed to Ts'ui Shih (*c.* 100–170) [whose familiy had once owned large areas of land] set out an ideal and doubtless stylised programme of the different occupations of the farmer and his household for the 12 months of the year. Although the author's family came from the north-east (near the modern Peking [Beijing]), the text was probably written with the conditions of Lo-yang [city in northwest China, capital of the twelfth-century B.C. Chou dynasty] in mind.

The Ts'ui family had been land-owners, but by the second century A.D. their fortunes were not what they had been. Indeed, the expenses incurred in providing his father with a suitable funeral and in having a proper set of monuments erected left Ts'ui Shih in a state of penury, and he was forced at one time to earn a living in the much despised liquor trade. At a later stage in his life, when he went to serve as a provincial governor in the north, Ts'ui Shih came face to face with the conditions of poverty from the other side of the fence. The district was well-suited to the growth of hemp, but the new governor was shocked to find that the inhabitants used grasses as a protection against the cold and that textile-weaving was hardly known. Ts'ui Shih soon saw to it that the necessary equipment and instruction was provided so that locally woven textiles could be worn.

His set of rules for husbandry are concerned with a variety of subjects, which range from religious festivals and education to domestic economy and the preparation of remedies for sickness. The farmer is told when he should plant, weed and harvest his various crops; and his womenfolk when they should set in motion the different processes of silk-production, weaving, dyeing and tailoring. There is a set programme for processing foods, gathering wild plants and distilling their drugs for medicines; and for the maintenance of property and the care of domestic and farming equipment. The head of the family is advised when he should send his youngsters off to school, and at what times of the year it is favourable to buy in the stores that he needs, or to sell his own produce.

The book starts with instructions for keeping the festival of the New Year's Day, on the first day of the first month [toward the middle of our February]. The whole family must purify themselves before the offerings of strong drink may be presented at the shrine; and once this part of the ceremony was over, all members, senior and junior alike, should gather in their appointed places of precedence to sit in attendance before their ancestors. Women and children, sons and grandsons duly presented

Edict of Emperor Wen on the Importance of Agriculture (163 B.C.)

Emperor Wen, who reigned from 180–157 B.C., was one of many Chinese rulers who appreciated how important agriculture was to imperial Chinese society. In the following edict, he expresses concern about the state of the agricultural economy. Thereafter, farmers could exchange gifts of grain to the imperial government for honorary titles or pardons from criminal punishments. The system effectively boosted agricultural production for the term of Wen's reign.

For the past several years there have been no good harvests, and our people have suffered the calamities of flood, drought, and pestilence. We are deeply grieved by this, but being ignorant and unenlightened, we have been unable to discover where the blame lies. We have considered whether our administration has been guilty of some error or our actions of some fault. Have we failed to follow the Way of Heaven or to obtain the benefits of Earth? Have we caused disharmony in human affairs or neglected the gods that they do not accept our offerings? What has brought on these things? Have the provisions for our officials been too lavish or have we indulged in too many unprofitable affairs? Why is the food of the people so scarce? When the fields are surveyed, they have not decreased, and when the people are counted they have not grown in number, so that the amount of land for each person is the same as before or even greater, And yet there is a drastic shortage of food. Where does the blame lie? Is it that too many people pursue secondary activities to the detriment of agriculture? Is it that too much grain is used to make wine or too many domestic animals are being raised? I have been unable to attain a proper balance between important and unimportant affairs. Let this matter be debated by the chancellor, the nobles, the high officials, and learned doctors. Let all exhaust their efforts and ponder deeply whether there is some way to aid the people. Let nothing be concealed from us!

Quoted in William Theodore de Bary and Irene Bloom, eds., *Sources of Chinese Tradition.* Vol. 1. New York: Columbia University Press, 1999.

themselves to the head of the family and raised their goblets in due solemnity. For this was one of the principal occasions of the year for the family to pray for happiness and prosperity; and a day could be suitably chosen to hold the ceremony of giving a youth his cap, as a means of showing his acceptance as an adult member of the community.

Seasonal Tasks

The first month was a season when the agricultural year had hardly begun, and the opportunity could be taken to send boys to school. But there were trees which could be transplanted, such as bamboo, pine or oak, or those that produced lacquer or oils; and a man could safely sow melons and gourds, onions and garlic. The decayed leaves should be swept up and the fields manured. Trees could be pruned, but bamboo and timber should not be felled.

There were other religious occasions during the year. In the second and eighth months offerings of leeks and eggs were presented to the lord of the soil and the spirits of the seasons; in the eighth month millet and piglets were to be reverently presented to the ancestral graves; and a whole host of rites which were to be performed in the twelfth month in honour of spirits and ancestors included the slaughter of pigs and sheep, fasting and purification, and offerings of wine. There were also the festivals that accompanied climatic changes such as the summer and winter solstices, as well as the spring festival of re-awakening. The first and twelfth months were the correct time for paying dutiful visits to one's social superiors; the second and third for a man to practise his archery, so that he would be ready to deal with robbers; and at the same time a man should repair his gates and doors for the protection of his household. In the ninth month a wise man would check the state of his weapons; and he should also spare a thought for the orphans, widows and sick members of the clan, and provide for their needs in the coming winter.

The Farmer's Year

Heavy ground was broken up in the first month; good arable in the second; and light sandy soils in the third; and in some of the fields this work might continue right through to the seventh month. Hay was cut in the fifth and eighth months, and the sixth month was the time for hoeing. For the first eight months of the year there was usually some crop or vegetable to be sown; in addition to cereals there were gourds, beans or hemp, and the right time depended on seasonal conditions, such as the rains of the third month or the summer solstice of the fifth month. There were a number of herbs to be collected and drugs to be compounded in the fifth month, when it was advisable to take certain hygienic precautions. For the *Yin* and the *Yang* [opposing but complementary forces representing female qualities (*Yin*) of gentleness and yielding, and male qualities (*Yang*) of assertiveness and force] were locked in combat, and it would be wise for man and wife to sleep in separate rooms.

Meanwhile the women of the household were busy nurturing their silk-worms and keeping careful watch over their life-cycle so that the threads could be used to best advantage. In the sixth month they would be spinning the textiles, before settling down to the summer tasks of washing old clothes, cutting new clothes and dyeing the silk cloth. In the tenth month they were best employed on working hemp and fashioning sandals; and there were few months in the year when the country household was not engaged in brewing liquors or preserving foods with the help of seasonings that had been gathered from the woods at the right time.

Spring was a time for re-plastering the walls of the house and applying a fresh coat of lacquer where this was suitable. In the fifth month a farmer should remember that the seasonal rains would soon turn the lanes into an impassable quagmire, and it would be prudent to lay in a supply of food and firewood. It was also a time to buy a supply of wheat-bran, which should be dried and stored in jars. These needed to be sealed carefully so that they did not breed maggots; and come the winter the supply could be used as fodder for the horses. Granaries and storage pits should be repaired in the ninth month; and at the end of the year the far-sighted farmer would assemble his plough for the coming year's work and take care to feed his oxen to their fill, so that they would be fit and strong to face the labour of the working year that lay ahead.

Biography of a Merchant in the Ming Dynasty

Wang Tao-k'un

While the imperial Chinese venerated agricultural workers as productive members of society, they considered merchants, whose livelihood depended on squeezing profits from the people, at best questionable and at worst immoral. As the imperial age progressed, many merchants amassed great fortunes and earned a reputation for exploiting the poor. Some merchants, however, were acknowledged for their high principles, and one sixteenth-century official, Wang Tao-k'un (1523–1593), wrote biographies of notable merchants in defense of the blighted profession. In the following extract, Wang Tao-k'un, whose ancestors were salt merchants, describes the achievements of Mr. Wang, a successful merchant who showed concern for social justice and the plight of the less fortunate.

In 1556, Mr. Wang, who was ninety years old at the time, was given the highest prefectural [honorary regional government] title by imperial decree and from that time on has been treated with the courtesies due an elder. As the histories testify, in ancient times emperors often honored venerable old men so as to receive the benefit of their constant advice. Even at his great age Mr. Wang is a man of the highest integrity; therefore I now extol his deeds in order to show my respect for virtuous old men.

Mr. Wang's formal name is T'ung-pao and polite name Ch'u-ch'uan. He is from Yen township of She county [in Shang-hai]. His ancestors were originally from T'an-mo [township] but a number of them split away from the family and moved to Yen township. (It is said that Mr. Wang and I are descended from a

Wang Tao-k'un, "The Biography of Gentleman Wang," *Chinese Civilization and Society: A Sourcebook,* edited by Patricia Buckley Ebrey. New York: The Free Press, 1981.

common ancestor.) Even as a teenager, he was famous for his skill in making money.

Mr. Wang lives in Shang-hai. Being open and confident he has attracted the respect of many capable and prosperous people who compete to attach themselves to him. At first, Mr. Wang's capital was no greater than the average person's. Later, as he grew more prosperous every day, the number of his associates also steadily increased. To accommodate his apprentices, Mr. Wang built buildings with doors on four sides. Whenever customers came, they could be taken care of from all four directions; thus, no one ever had to wait very long.

Mr. Wang set up the following guidelines for his associates: do not let anyone who lives in another county control the banking; when lending money, never harass law-abiding people unnecessarily or give them less than they need; charge low interest on loans; do not aim at high profit and do not ask for daily interest. These principles led customers to throng to him, even ones from neighboring towns and provinces. Within a short time, Mr. Wang accumulated great wealth; in fact, of all the rich people in that area he became the richest.

Philanthropy

Mr. Wang liked to help people and to give assistance to the poor. If anyone among his kinsmen could not afford a funeral for his parents, Mr. Wang would always buy some land and build a tomb for him. As soon as he heard someone could not make ends meet, he would buy land to rent to him. Whenever he was out traveling and met some unburied spirit, he would bid his servants bury it and present some offerings.

During the Chia-ching period [1521–1567], there was a serious drought, and the Prefect [government official] proposed opening the granary. Considering the hardship this would cause the people, Mr. Wang sent a written report to the Prefect, as follows:

> This proposal will cause starving people to travel here from hundreds of *li* away to wait for the distribution. Even if there are no delays en route, they may die before they get here. Yet if we make them stay home and wait for a pint of food, it will be like abandoning them to die in the gutters. I suggest that we exchange the grain for money and distribute it around the area. All the wealthy

people ought to donate some money to help the poor. I myself will start with a donation of a hundred taels [chinese coin, one tael equalled 1⅓ ounces of silver] of gold.

The Prefect accepted his suggestion and everyone said that this was much more convenient. Then Mr. Wang also prepared some food to feed people in his own county and caused similar actions to be taken throughout the whole of Shang-hai. Thus most people in this area survived.

Once Tung-ching Bridge in Wu-hui [in modern-day Hong Kong] was damaged and Mr. Wang donated a hundred strings of cash for repairs. From then on, whenever a dike or bridge was built, he would donate a similar sum to promote such community activities.

Religious Conviction

Mr. Wang once had a dream in which three Taoist priests approached his house. And, indeed, the next day he received a picture which matched his dream. He regarded the priests as gods and worshipped them sincerely. Later he was almost poisoned but escaped the disaster by tipping over the poison. Another time when he was traveling from Tan-yang [a town near Beijing] the driver, with evil intentions, was leading him down the wrong road. Fortunately, he met an old man who cautioned him and he escaped. Mr. Wang himself said that it must have been because of the gods' help that he survived each time. Hence, he spent several thousand taels of gold to construct a Three Taoist Temple near Mt. Lion [in Yunnan province, southwest China]. This was reported to Emperor Shih-tsung, who conferred a tablet upon the temple with these words on it: "A divine manifestation." The local people have recourse to this temple in cases of flood, drought, disease, and suffering.

When some bullies encroached upon the ancestral temple on Mount Ling and occupied his ancestral cemetery in Yeh village, Mr. Wang repaired all the damage, sparing no expense; thereafter, everyone praised him as a righteous man.

Man of Wisdom

When the "Island barbarians" [pirates from Japan] raided Shang-hai, some of Mr. Wang's associates fled with his money. Nevertheless, he remained unmoved and made no inquiries. Neighbors came to see him, saying, "Mr. Wang, please cheer up. Really this loss is as insignificant as plucking a hair out of a horse's skin."

Mr. Wang smiled and replied, "Where can the hair grow when there's no skin left? When these people first came to join me, it was unexpected; now that they have gone, I myself remain unchanged and bear no resentment." Within a short time, his business revived; yet Mr. Wang still remained unmoved. Hence, people said that he was a man of wisdom because neither success nor frustration could affect him.

Whenever there was a dispute, Mr. Wang could always resolve it immediately, even if it was quite serious. When Magistrate Hsü was in charge of Shang-hai, he imprisoned someone named Chu, who died in jail. The victim's father then presented a petition to the Emperor which worried the Magistrate. The officials, elders, and local leaders were willing to offer the father a thousand taels of gold on the Magistrate's behalf, but on discussing it, they decided only Mr. Wang could settle the matter, and indeed he persuaded the father to accept the terms. Then the Magistrate was transferred to another position. Upon learning this fact, the officials, elders, and local leaders all quickly dispersed. Mr. Wang sighed and said, "It isn't easy to collect a thousand taels of gold but I will not break the promise made to the Magistrate in trouble." He then paid the thousand taels of gold and the Magistrate was out of his difficulties. Even when Magistrate Hsü was dismissed soon thereafter, Mr. Wang did not voice any concern, and after two years Hsü returned the thousand taels of gold to him.

Instruction from Heaven

Later when Mr. Chu set up dikes, a dispute occurred which involved thousands of people. The official tried to straighten out the merits of the case, but still it could not be resolved. Therefore the official asked Mr. Wang to take a hand in the matter. He successfully mediated the dispute merely by sending out a long letter. Later he was singled out to promote good community relations in Lin-ho and resolved all the quarrels there. Thus everybody praised him, saying, "Mr. Wang is capable of mediating disputes. He has the manner of a gentleman of national stature, and even the gentlemen of antiquity were not his equals."

When Mr. Wang is at home he is always in high spirits. He likes to make friends with the chivalrous youths. In his later years he has become particularly fond of chess, often staying up all night until he either wins or loses a game. The youths say that Mr. Wang is no ordinary person, that he must have received instruction from Heaven.

Now Mr. Wang is almost one hundred years old. He has at least thirty sons and grandsons living at home with him. It is said, "One who seeks perfection will attain it." This describes Mr. Wang perfectly.

The Palace Eunuchs

Mary M. Anderson

In imperial China, where high infant mortality was the rule, emperors kept thousands of wives and concubines to ensure many heirs to the throne. In order to protect the purity of the imperial line, eunuchs, males who were rendered sexually impotent, were employed to guard the chastity of the women who lived their entire lives within the palace walls (known as the "Great Within"). Eunuchs were also charged with preserving the aura of sacredness and secrecy that surrounded the emperor. As the emperor's right to rule rested on a mandate from heaven that demanded scrupulous personal conduct, rulers relied upon eunuchs' discretion not to reveal their human foibles. Historians report, however, that on many occasions this trust was misplaced, and eunuchs became embroiled in palace intrigues that in some cases contributed to the fall of China's great dynasties.

In the following extract from *Hidden Power: The Palace Eunuchs of Imperial China*, author Mary M. Anderson describes how eunuchs were rendered impotent and the varied jobs they did in the imperial palace. She says they were treated harshly, particularly in view of their gentle and sensitive natures. Anderson, an author who has lived in the Orient and written about Eastern culture and traditions, also wrote *The Festivals of Nepal* (1971).

E very fifth year, each princely son was required to furnish the Manchu palace [of the Ming dynasty (1368–1644)] with eight young eunuchs who had been well trained, inspected for proper castration, and declared free of disease or uncleanliness in person. The palace paid 250 taels [chinese coin; one tael equals 1⅓ ounces of silver] to the princes for purchasing and training each eunuch. Since this system did not nearly supply the numbers of eunuchs required by the palace, grown men could voluntarily have themselves castrated, but to be accepted for service at the palace, they had to find someone to vouch for their character, and they invariably ended up with menial jobs that did not necessitate entrance into the imperial ladies' apartments. Large numbers of young boys, purchased from their families, were castrated and drafted into the palace where they were especially favored by harem ladies as pets and companions.

All eunuchs were thought of as "pure," but those under ten years of age were termed "thoroughly pure." These were prized by palace ladies and given as much freedom and familiarity as if they were girls, and allowed to perform bedroom and bathroom duties of the most intimate nature. Boy eunuchs were supposedly free of any licentiousness, even in thought. As they grew older they were replaced by younger eunuchs and given duties outside the ladies' quarters.

Just outside the Forbidden City [imperial palace] gate, but within the Imperial City, was a run-down building where several "knifers,"—who were recognized by the government as qualified to perform castrations, though they received no government salary, plied their trade. Theirs was a hereditary, family profession. They collected six taels for each surgery and nursing the eunuch through the initial stage of recovery.

Surgery and Recovery

When the surgery was about to take place, the candidate was placed on a low bed in a semi-reclining position, and asked once more if he would ever regret being castrated. If the answer was no, one man clasped him about the waist while two others separated his legs and held them firmly down to prevent any movement. Tight bandages were wound around the thighs and lower abdomen, the patient was given a bowl of nerve-stunning herbal tea, and his private parts were desensitized with baths of hot pepper water. Both penis and testicles were then swiftly cut off with a small curved knife as closely as possible to the body. A metal plug was immediately inserted into the urethra, and the entire wound covered with water-soaked paper and carefully bandaged. Immediately thereafter, the eunuch was made to walk about the room for two or three hours supported on each side by the "knifers" before he was allowed to lie down. He was not allowed to drink any liquid for three days, during which time he suffered great agony from thirst and extreme pain, and was unable to urinate. At the end of three days, the bandages were removed, the inserted plug pulled out, and hopefully the sufferer was able to obtain relief with a copious flow of urine, at which time he was congratulated and considered out of danger. If the surgery rendered the eunuch unable to urinate, the passages having grown closed, he was doomed to an agonizing death.

It is claimed that eunuchs rarely died from the crude surgery, only about two cases in a hundred proving fatal. This is not difficult to believe, for if the fatality rate had been high, it is unlikely that thousands of males would have chosen this means to try to improve their economic status.

Move to the Imperial Palace

When thoroughly recovered, usually in two or three months, and after perhaps a year of training in princely establishments, they were transferred to the imperial palace where they were again closely examined by old, experienced eunuchs to ascertain that they had been rendered completely sexless.

The severed parts, euphemistically called the *pao*, meaning the "precious," were preserved in a hermetically sealed vessel, and were highly valued by the eunuch. They were always placed on a high shelf to symbolize that the owner should rise to high rank. The eunuch also treasured his "precious" because, to be promoted to a higher grade, he was obliged to first display his emasculated parts and be reexamined by the chief eunuch. If his "Precious" should be lost or stolen, at promotion time he had to buy one from the eunuch clinic, or he could borrow or rent one from another eunuch. It was also vital that the eunuch's organs be placed in his coffin at his death in the hope of hoodwinking the gods of the underworld into believing that he was a complete man: otherwise he was doomed to appeal in the next world as a she-male.

Besides the hundreds and sometimes thousands of eunuchs employed in household and harem duties, a few were "ordained" to become one of the eighteen Lamaist [Buddhist] priests which the palace maintained expressly to attend to the spiritual welfare of the female inmates. Though often as not the chosen eunuchs could neither read nor write and knew nothing about the craft of priesthood they earned a double salary. Needless to say, vacancies among the eunuch lamas were filled without delay.

Another some 300 eunuchs were employed as actors and singers in the ever popular palace theatricals. Eunuch performers lived outside the palace in the Imperial City on small salaries, but were accustomed to receive gratuities from their imperial audiences for especially pleasing performances.

Harsh Treatment and Meager Salaries

Eunuchs who ran away from the palace were invariably caught by special police and returned to the Forbidden City. First-time offenders were imprisoned for two months, given twenty blows of the bamboo or whip, and sent back to duty. Those who deserted a second time were put in a *cangue* for two months—a large wooden frame that clamped around the neck, preventing lying down or feeding oneself. Third time defectors were banished to Manchuria for two-and-a-half years, as were eunuchs who were caught in thievery. If the stolen goods were valued by the emperor, however, the offender was beheaded at a special grounds about ten miles from Peking. Neglect of duty or laziness were punished by whippings. The chief eunuch summoned one eunuch from each of the forty-eight household departments to administer the whipping with bamboo rods. The culprit received 80 to 100 blows and was then sent to a doctor—also eunuch—to have the wounds dressed. After three days, the offender was again flogged, in a punishment called "raising the scabs."

Eunuch salaries in the late 1800s usually ranged from two to four taels a month. Twelve taels was the highest pay allowed to eunuchs of any rank. In addition, each eunuch received a quantity of rice each month. Groups of eunuchs banded together to organize messes, each donating food as needed. The cooking was done in the palace kitchens. The eunuchs lived in small huts, called "menials' houses," attached to the sides of main buildings where their employers resided and where the eunuchs could be readily summoned. Each of the myriad of courtyards in the Forbidden City had a colony of eunuchs.

Palace eunuchs were allowed to worship in the temples, to burn incense, practice fasting, and donate money and offerings, but they were prohibited from ascending the altar of the main deity, as were all cripples, deformed persons, those lacking an eye, limb, or any other body part, and menstruating females.

Geishas in Imperial China

Eunuchs of the imperial palace were only one social group who lived out of the mainstream of Chinese society. Chinese geishas, trained from childhood to serve the sexual needs of upper-class men, were also known to lead colorful lives that flaunted traditional social norms and values. Historian Victoria Cass describes the life of Xue Susu, a notorious geisha of the Ming dynasty.

One woman of the late Ming typified this colorful warrior-geisha: the famous artist Xue Susu. In her life we see encapsulated many of the features of these dramatic women of the geisha class. Xue, like many of the geishas of high status, was a painter; one of her scrolls has been ranked as "the most accomplished work of its kind in the whole of the Ming period." Scholars have claimed her brushwork is "vigorous and forceful," calling her a "master of technique." Xue was established as a mate in excellence as well; she lived at different times with some of the most important intellectuals of the late Ming.

Besides her painting, Xue was famous for her flamboyantly defiant romanticism; she was one of the most charismatic women of the Ming. One intellectual thought she was extraordinary: "Xue Susu has a spirit that is heroic. She values herself highly, and does not receive common people, but only the learned and intelligent"; and another noted that she deliberately took her name from a famous female warrior of the past. . . .

Nothing demonstrates the charismatic nature of these women more than the exceptional sport to which Xue Susu dedicated herself. Xue was an expert in mounted archery, and she loved to prove it. Qian Qianyi [seventeenth-century poet] tells us that "as a child Xue Susu lived in Beijing for a time; and out in the suburbs she practiced the arts of the mounted archer." The geisha then continued her training and eventually became famous for her exhibitions. . . . The thrill of enjoying her performance was captured by the poet Lu Bi:

The Song of Watching Susu Shoot the Arrows

As the wine grows sweet we ask her now to perform the arrow-shoot.
With her hair tied back and her single-layer shirt, she hesitates now before the shot.
The fine bindings and her red sleeves exposed now to show her armlet and glove.
She tips her head to measure the shot; and beneath her cloudlike tresses now,
Both her shoulders square back.

Victoria Cass, *Dangerous Women: Warriors, Grannies, and Geishas of the Ming.* New York: Roman & Littlefield, 1999.

Physical Traits and Personalities of Eunuchs

Eunuchs were easily recognizable by their high falsetto voices (for which they were derisively called "crows"), as well as their want of beards, their cringing, hang-dog demeanor, and often their bloated appearance—though in old age they invariably became thin and deeply wrinkled, making them look like old women. Low-ranking eunuchs wore a long grey robe under a shorter dark blue coat, and had to wear their official hats and boots when on duty. In olden times, high-ranking palace eunuchs wore ornate robes of brilliantly embroidered colors.

Eunuchs had such a peculiar walk that they could easily be recognized at great distances. They characteristically leaned slightly forward, their legs close together, taking short, mincing steps, with the toes turned outward. Whether this odd walk was a physical necessity, or was imposed upon eunuchs as a rule of conduct to denote the eunuch's station is not known. For a long time after castration, many young eunuchs wet their beds and themselves. No notice of this was taken for a time, but a long continuance of the problem resulted in severe floggings, which were continued until the habit was broken or outgrown. Thus, the Chinese spoke of them behind their backs as "stinking eunuchs," and claimed they could smell one a mile and a half away. A common expression used for a normal person who offended the nose was, "He's smelly as a eunuch." The most common and vulgar name for a eunuch was "Old Earl" or "Old Rooster," insulting terms that were never used to the eunuch's face. Eunuchs were so extremely sensitive to any reference to their deficiency, it is said, that such items as a spoutless teapot or a tailless dog were never mentioned in their presence.

Most of the eunuchs' leisure time was spent in gambling among themselves, their greatest source of enjoyment. It is said they were especially affectionate toward women and children, and loved pets, many of them keeping a puppy on which they lavished great affection. As late as the 1920s, one dismissed but fairly well-off eunuch was commonly seen ice-skating on Peking's outdoor rink, displaying miniature Chinese dogs that he sold to foreign ladies to make his living.

The Arts and Entertainment

CHAPTER
4

Chapter Preface

Cultural values were transmitted to the illiterate rural peasants of imperial China through arts and entertainment. Actors, opera singers, street entertainers, and storytellers conveyed Confucian and Buddhist moral treatises in story and song, known to provoke strong emotions in their audience. Values were also transmitted through the art of landscape painters who sought to develop the moral character of their viewers to promote "harmony between heaven and earth." However, artistic expression in imperial China also gave people a means to escape the social conventions and the rigors of daily life, and to enter the world of the imagination. At times arts and entertainment even served as a venue for veiled social protest.

The oral tradition contained a rich reservoir of Confucian, Taoist, and Buddhist moral tales that were regularly told in towns and villages during Chinese festivals by costumed storytellers, actors, and singers. Accompanied by the piercing discords of Chinese flutes, xylophones, guitars, and deep bass drums, the stories, plays, and operas focused on themes of children's duty to their parents, marital fidelity, and family relationships. In one famous opera, *Mulian Rescues His Mother*, the young hero braves great danger en route to the underworld to rescue his mother's soul, which had been condemned for her sins of infidelity, greed, and blasphemy. Performed both in the imperial palace and in rural villages, the story reinforced the values of filial piety (duty to parents) and the inferiority of women.

Chinese banquets, which accompanied all festive occasions, served to reinforce the Confucian value of hierarchy. Rules dictated by imperial decree detailed the correct ways to prepare and serve food for ceremonies at each level of society. As one moved up the social scale, these became more elaborate and exacting. While villagers complied with rules for serving simple meals of pork, fish, and rice, the emperor had to follow strict regulations on how his guests should be fed at imperial banquets. For example, during the tenth-century Song dynasty, high officials were served eleven courses and limitless wine at the imperial palace; officials of the middle ranks were given seven courses and five pitchers of wine; and the lower rank officials received three courses and one jug of wine. At the great imperial banquets for foreign dignitaries, these guests were honored with many more courses served according to strict protocol. One Chinese account from the eleventh century describes the precise serving order of more than two hundred dishes at one of these great imperial banquets:

> [The feast began with] forty-one dishes of pigs, snails, pork, goose, duck, mutton, pigeon, fried, sauteed, grilled, roast on the spit, roast in the oven or boiled; forty-two dishes based on fruits and sweet meats; twenty dishes of vegetable; nine of boiled rice served with different ingredients . . . ; twenty-nine dishes of dried fish; seventeen refreshments (li-chee juice, honey or ginger drinks, paw-paw juice . . .); nineteen kinds of pie and fifty-seven desserts.

The hierarchical values of imperial society were also reflected in the world of the Chinese artist. In his treatise instructing landscape painters, the eleventh-century artist Kuo Hsi likened a mountain, the subject of many Chinese paintings, to "an emperor sitting majestically in all his glory . . . giving audience to his subjects, without sign or arrogance or haughtiness." Another famous eleventh-century landscape artist, Jing Hao, wrote guidelines for artists that called on them to imbue their work with "harmony" to encourage a feeling of unity with the cosmos and acceptance of one's place in the social hierarchy.

Although arts and entertainment reinforced the norms and values of imperial society, they also provided a temporary reprieve from the many duties, obligations, and social distinctions characteristic of Confucian life. Street entertainers attracted people from all social classes. The rich and the poor intermingled and enjoyed satires that made fun of the ancient sages or mocked the corruption or inefficiency of bureaucratic officials. Performers in village operas encouraged peasants to vent their frustrations at the heartlessness of the privileged classes or the inhumanity of local officials. The arts, therefore, could serve as a vehicle of social protest. They could also provide an outlet for people to temporarily escape the difficulties of daily existence and enter the more perfect world of the imagination. Guo Xi described the natural human desire for wish fulfillment well when he said:

It is human nature to resent the hustle and bustle of society, and to wish to see, but not always succeed in seeing, immortals hidden in the clouds. . . . Now the artist has reproduced it for us. One can imagine oneself sitting on rocks in a gully hearing the cries of monkeys and birds; while in one's own sitting room the light of the mountains and the colors of the water dazzle one's eyes. Is it not a joy, a fulfillment of one's dream?

In both reinforcing Chinese culture and providing an acceptable avenue for people to express frustrations with the imperial order, the arts and entertainment helped to maintain the balance and harmony so highly prized by Chinese civilization.

Amusements in Thirteenth-Century Imperial China

Jacques Gernet

In the thriving metropolis of Hangzhou (Hangchow), the Chinese capital at the close of the Southern Song dynasty in the late thirteenth century, people of all classes had a great appetite for entertainment and amusements. In the following extract from *Daily Life in China on the Eve of the Mongol Invasion, 1250–1276*, French scholar Jacques Gernet describes how rich and poor people abandoned the usual formalities customary in the stratified society of imperial China when they came together to watch actors, acrobats, jugglers, puppeteers, boxers, storytellers, performing fish, snake charmers, and other entertainers in one of the many gathering places in Hangzhou. Originally published in France in 1959, Gernet's book is based almost entirely on his own translations of original Chinese texts and is considered a classic work on the everyday lives of people in imperial China. Gernet is also the author of *Ancient China from the Beginnings to the Empire* (1968) and *China and the Christian Impact: A Conflict of Cultures* (1985).

There was an aura of magic and religion about the arts and about all forms of play [in imperial China]: it was on religious occasions that people gave themselves up to play activities, and the aims and character of the games they played went back to very early times when magic had given them a practical or a dramatic function. Vestiges of these origins still survived in T'ang times [618–907] but the growth of the towns under the Sung [dynasty, 960–1279] resulted in a secularization of games and of the arts more complete than had been the case after earlier social changes, which removed any vestiges of magico-religious thought and content.

Jacques Gernet, *Daily Life in China on the Eve of the Mongol Invasion, 1250–1276*. Stanford, CA: Stanford University Press, 1962.

As the rise of new social strata in the town (rich and petty traders, the urban lower classes) made itself felt, so also new needs arose in the matter of the arts and of amusements. Many types of popular entertainers appeared, and . . . the 'entertainment industry' employed a considerable proportion of the common people in Hangchow. It was no longer only in aristocratic and court circles that, as had traditionally been the custom since earliest times in China, jugglers, mountebanks [charlatans], musicians and storytellers exhibited their talents, but they also did so in the middle of the streets, before an audience in which merchants mingled with the common people. The repertoire, the type of entertainment and the style of the performance varied according to the audience, but at the same time there was mutual borrowing between the amusements of the upper and of the lower classes which resulted in their becoming more or less the same. . . .

The big cities, and Hangchow more than any of them, because of the density of its population and the mixture of classes in it, had increased the opportunities for contact between different kinds of people and had intensified relations between them. . . .

Pleasure Grounds

Hangchow was full of places for social gatherings of one kind or another: the gardens outside the ramparts where the townspeople went for pleasure outings, odd spaces or street-corners where a gaping crowd collected round some acrobat, tea-houses where rich people went to take lessons in playing musical instruments, boats on the lake where guests were entertained. . . . But Hangchow had its places of amusement that were specifically designed as such. These were the special 'pleasure grounds', a kind of vast covered market where lessons were given in dramatic art and in singing and music, and where theatrical representations of all kinds could be seen daily. The name given to these establishments signified, according to the interpretation given by contemporaries, that they were places 'where no one stood on ceremony', that is to say, that people of all sorts and conditions could rub shoulders with each other there without bothering about the usual rites and formalities. There had already been bazaars of this kind in Kaifeng, the Northern Sung capital, at the beginning of the twelfth century. The first to be constructed in

Hangchow dated from the reign-period known as the Restoration of Sung (1131–1162), and they were instituted for the soldiers garrisoned in the city, most of whom, being natives of the northern provinces, were separated from their families, and must have been at a loss to know how to fill their leisure hours.

The imperial government staffed these pleasure grounds with singing-girls and women-musicians, and to begin with, the function of these bazaars was to provide brothels for the soldiers. 'Nowadays,' writes an author in 1275, 'these establishments have become places of debauch and of perdition for society people and young men of good social standing.' At that time there were seventeen or twenty-three (different sources give different numbers) of these pleasure grounds in Hangchow, most of them outside the ramparts, near the gates of the city. Those in the suburbs were not controlled by the same branch of the administration which controlled those in the city proper, but all of them had a State official in charge.

The pleasure grounds contained various instruction centres—thirteen in all—giving tuition in drama and music. Each one had its 'head' or 'director', and the artistes wore costumes which varied according to what group they belonged to and what their rank and classification were. They might wear violet and purple, red and blue, or sometimes a full skirt with yellow edging. The actors wore turbans of various shapes and colours, the musicians caps. Depending upon which section they belonged to, the musicians played the sad-sounding flute originating from Central Asia, the Chinese transverse flute, the 'great drum', a xylophone with six or nine elements as big as the palm of a hand, joined together with a leather thong, the four-stringed guitar, the guitar in the form of a long flat rectangle with three strings, pan-pipes with thirteen reeds, the body of which was made of a dried calabash, and an instrument similar to the xylophone but with plates made of metal or stone.

Street Theatre

In other groups, various types of singing were taught, as well as dancing and dramatic art. The drama made quite a feature of short farcical scenes, acrobatic turns and satirical sketches. There were actors who imitated the peasants of Shantung and Hopei [in northern China] for this type of comedy had been much in vogue at Kaifeng and was kept up in Hangchow. Other scenes were in the form of a ballet accompanied with songs and instrumental music. There were also Chinese shadow plays, in which the actors were puppets cut out of paper with articulated joints, and various other kinds of marionette theatres featuring puppets on strings pulled from above or on sticks manipulated from below, or 'live' ones played by families of actors with thin, graceful limbs. The puppeteers who worked the articulated puppets made them speak in a shrill, nasal voice. Both shadows and puppets acted little scenes: stories of ghosts and marvels, crime stories, and romantic pieces in which history mingled with fiction. Storytellers were also popular. They all specialized in one or other type of story: tales of genies and demons, stories about shrewd judges who were particularly clever at resolving the most baffling cases, tales of battle in which the heroes showed superhuman strength and skill, Buddhist stories recounting episodes in former lives of the Buddha. Both plays and stories inclined at times to social satire and denounced the corrupt practices of those in power.

Acrobats and Unusual Acts

Acrobats and jugglers were also to be seen in the pleasure grounds, but usually they gave their shows on the fringes of these places, in spaces marked off on the pavements by barriers. At the northern pleasure ground, near one of the bridges over which the Imperial Way ran, there were thirteen of such 'barriers'. But entertainers did not confine themselves to these spaces which were apparently specially reserved for them; they were to be seen at crossroads, in the squares and in the markets—anywhere, in fact, where they could collect a crowd. Sometimes they put up temporary shelters made of bamboo stakes and mats. Thus right in the middle of the streets passers-by could marvel at acrobats with their heads between their legs, tightrope walkers with poles on their shoulders from which hung jars of water full to the brim, not a drop of which was spilled as they walked their rope, men juggling with plates, bottles or large jugs, men exhibiting bears or performing ants, sword-swallowers, wrestlers or boxers. Groups of from three to five musicians went about singing and dancing while balancing on their shoulders one or two little boys and girls. Storytellers and men who asked riddles also drew crowds, humorists too 'who gave absurd commentaries on the solemn Classics and demonstrated, by means of erudite wordplay, that the Buddha, Lao-tzu [founder of the Chinese religion of Taoism] and Confucius were women'.

An author at the end of the thirteenth century gives the following description of the various curious spectacles he had seen

Street Vendors in Thirteenth-Century China

In the following extract from the thirteenth-century drama, Pai-hua t'ing, *an actor dressed as a street vendor calls to his potential customers. The passage is evidence of the pleasure the imperial Chinese took in food.*

Fruits on sticks for sale, fruits on sticks for sale! I've just left the tile districts [pleasure quarters], departed the tea houses to swiftly pass the pleasureland of kingfisher green and worldly red to enter the district of orioles and flowers. . . . This fruit is homegrown, just picked. There are juicy-juicy-sweet, full-full-fragrant, sweet-smelling, red and watery fresh-peeled round-eye lichees from Fu-chou; from P'ing-chiang [Su-chou] some sour-sour-tart, shady-cool, sweet-sweet-luscious, yellow oranges and green tangerines with the leaves still on; there're some supple-supple-soft, quite-quite-white, crystal-sweet, crushed-flat candied persimmons from Sung-yang; from Wu-chou I have snappy-snappy-crisp, juicy-juicy-fresh, glitter-glitter-bright dragon-twined jujubes kneaded in sugar; there are ginger threads from Hsin-chien split fine and dipped in honey sugar as well as Kao-yu water caltrops wrinkled by the sun, dried by the wind and skinned; I have the blackest of black, reddest of red fingertip-size large melon seeds gathered in Wei; from Hsüan-ch'eng some half-sour, half-sweet, half-sweet, half-sour soft peaches skewered just right. I can't exhaust the list, so I'll lay out several kinds before your eyes. Oh, you sweet elegant ladies, beautiful women from fragrant chambers and embroidered kiosks; great and noble gentlemen from high halls and great buildings—I'm not just bragging to make false claims, but try mine and you'll forsake all others. You'll be sure to buy them once you try them. Oh! Sticks of fruit for sale.

Quoted in Frederick W. Mote, "Yuan and Ming," *Food in Chinese Culture,* ed. K.C. Chang. New Haven, CT: Yale University Press, 1977.

in Hangchow in his childhood. 'Here is a man showing performing fish: he has a large lacquer bowl in front of him in which
swim turtles, turbots and other fish. He beats time on a small
bronze gong and calls up one of the creatures by name. It comes
immediately and dances on the surface, wearing a kind of little
hat on its head. When it has finished its turn, it dives down again,
and the man calls another one. There is also the archery expert
who sets up in front of the spectators a big wheel a yard and a half
in diameter with all sorts of objects, flowers, birds and people
painted on it. He announces that he is going to hit this or that object on the target, and having started it spinning rapidly, he shoots
his arrows through the midst of the spectators. He hits the exact
spot he has declared he will hit. He can even score a hit on the
most precisely defined spots of the spinning target, such as a particular feather in a particular wing of a bird'. But apparently, adds
the author, he was not able to transmit his art to anyone. Another
entertainer is the snake-charmer who sits outside the Supreme
Temple [built in 1227 during the Yuari dynasty] and who has only
four fingers left. He will hold the strangest and most venomous
snakes in his hand as if they were nothing but eels. If a snake remains hidden in its basket and lends a deaf ear, its master blows
into a little pipe, and the snake comes to him immediately. This
curious person has trained several dozen different kinds of snakes,
some of them very large and dangerous; he keeps them in bamboo baskets. He can do whatever he likes with them, and the
practice of his craft has made him quite well off. The same author
also mentions a Taoist hermit who can be met with on the banks
of the river carrying on his back a creel full of shell-fish of various kinds and colours, all of them hypnotized.

Boxing Matches

But it was above all at festival times, when the entire population
of the town made merry in the streets and spent day and night
drinking and wandering about seeking for amusement, that
open-air entertainments were most numerous. When sacrifices
were offered at the Sacred Palace, ceremonies performed at the
altar in the southern suburbs, or imperial amnesties declared at
the Gate of Elegant Rectitude, shows and games of all kinds were
held all over the town. Boxing matches were held between the

Left and the Right Armies of the Imperial Guard on the Emperor's birthday and when banquets were held at the court. The strongest soldiers were picked out as boxers and their names placed on a special list. It was they who preceded the imperial chariot on the occasion of the ceremonies at the altar in the southern suburbs and on other occasions when sacrifices of the official cult [of the emperor] were performed. A hundred and twenty of them, bewhiskered and wearing caps on top of their long hair that floated round their shoulders, made a cordon on each side of the official route holding each other by the wrist. As for the boxers that were to be found in the pleasure grounds and contiguous pavement spaces, they were travelling performers who gave shows in all the towns. Coming from all the prefectures in the empire, they gathered at the Protection-of-the-kingdom monastery, on the South Peak, for the big boxing competitions that were periodically held there. The winner was awarded a flag, a silver cup, lengths of silk, a brocade robe, and a horse.

Entertaining the Elite

Most of the performers and entertainers who exhibited their talents in the pleasure grounds or in the streets gave performances in private mansions belonging to wealthy families, and sometimes even at the court, at festival times and when banquets were held. Or at least, if the performers were not the same, the performances were similar, although more skilful perhaps, more subtle, as befitted the more exacting and elegant tastes of this type of audience, than those in the pleasure grounds and markets, although there, too, people from the upper circles often mingled with the common people for the fun of keeping low company. . . . Some people with special gifts were permanently employed in rich households: chess-players, painters of chrysanthemums, writers of literary compositions, setters of amusing riddles. . . . These hangers-on were part of the household. Other artistes were hired to entertain the guests at big social gatherings: fashionable singing-girls, musicians, acrobats and conjurers.

It was only the most celebrated performers that were admitted into the presence of the Emperor. A text of 1280 lists fifty-five different varieties of performers, and gives the names of 554 of them who had given shows at the court towards the end of the Sung dynasty. Let us pick out a few of the different types from this varied list (some of the terms of which are difficult to interpret), to illustrate the extraordinary degree of specialization among entertainers: tellers of obscene stories, imitators of street cries, imitators of village talk, singers specializing in six different kinds of songs, sleight-of-hand experts, flyers of kites, ball players and footballers, archers and crossbow-men.

Village Opera: *Guo Buries His Son*

Transcribed by Sidney Gamble

In the villages of imperial China, elaborate operas with music, dance, and colorful costumes brought the classical texts to life for the largely illiterate rural Chinese masses. Stimulating the emotions of the audience, operas proved an effective means to transmit cultural values as well as give vent to villagers' frustration with social injustice.

The following extract is from a play popular in the provinces of northern China throughout the imperial age. Passed down through the oral tradition for hundreds of years, the play was based on a Confucian tract and tells of the heartlessness of the rich for the plight of the poor and the irreconcilable conflict between duty toward one's parents and love of one's child.

American social scientist Sidney Gamble (1890–1968) devoted his career to the study of everyday life in pre-revolutionary China. His best known work is *Peking: A Social Survey* (1921).

Guo Ju [a poor villager] *enters.*

Guo (*speaks*): Mother's illness is constantly on my mind. I am Guo Ju. Mother is very ill. I will go to her brother's house to borrow some rice to keep us going.

Guo (*sings*):

> Guo Ju sits in the front room, thinking about Mother's illness.
> Mother is bedridden; she would like a bowlful of rice, but there is none to give her.
> From her sickbed Mother tells me to go to her brother's house and borrow some.
> I bow and take my leave. I tell my wife to pay attention:
> If our mother gets cold, build up the fire for her;
> If our mother is thirsty, make some tea for her.
> Look—here is our rice bag; I am going to Uncle's to borrow some rice.
> Outside I look around; the street is filled with the well-to-do.
> I could take my bag into the main street to borrow rice, but the people there help the rich, not the poor.

Guo Buries His Son, transcribed by Sidney Gamble, 1929.

I'll use the small lanes, not the main street;

By crooked paths and devious ways I go through the *hutongs*
[alley ways]. . . .

[Guo Ju arrives at his Uncle's house and calls to him from his
gate.]

Uncle (*sings*):

I am just having a cup of wine in my inner chamber when suddenly I hear someone at the gate.

I put down the cup to see who has come.

I step outside my front hall and arrive at my gate.

Opening the gate I look up and see none other than my little
nephew Guo Ju.

We can't stand talking outside the gate, come with me to the
front hall.

Having spoken, I enter the gate. . . .

Guo (*sings*):

. . . Followed by Guo Ju, your little nephew.

Uncle (*sings*):

Sit here in the front hall.

Guo (*sings*):

He avoids me as he bows.

Having bowed, I take my seat.

May I ask whether you are well, Uncle, and Aunt also?

Uncle (*sings*):

I answer, "Fine, fine, fine"; and is my old sister well?

Guo (*sings*):

If you hadn't asked, it would have been all right, but now that
you have asked the tears pour down.

My mother is bedridden; she would like a bowl of rice, but
there is none to give her.

I wanted to make rice for her, but there is not even half a pint
of rice in the house.

I wanted to ask for a loan from someone who lives on the main
street, but most of them will help the rich, not the poor.

If you have rice, lend me a few pecks so I can take them home
and be a filial son.

If Mother recovers, I will never forget your generosity, Uncle.

What Guo Ju has said with a pure heart about borrowing
rice . . .

Uncle (*sings*):

What you have said I greatly dislike.

Three years ago you borrowed several pecks of rice from me,
and you have yet to repay half a pint.

You are asking again without having repaid what you owe—
where will I find the rice to give you?

The rice I have will feed my geese, ducks, pigs, and dogs, who
at least guard the house and announce the dawn.

The more I speak, the more I think and the angrier I get; the
dark fire of rage burns in my heart.

I pick up my walking stick and with hatred, hatred beat you to
death, you dog!

[Beats Guo Ju.]

Guo (*sings*):

Hear me, Uncle, with your hateful heart. This child has not
eaten for three meals, how can I fend off your great club?

I am humiliated, you savage, and I have a few things to say to
you!

I wouldn't have minded your refusing to lend us the rice; but
you ought not to have punished me so cruelly.

On hands and knees I anxiously scramble up from the ground.

I will leave having borrowed no rice, with nothing to offer
Mother at home.

Saying this I turn my face to tell you something else, Uncle:

Remember when we were rich and you were poor, and you
borrowed gold and silver from Guo Ju?

Now when you are rich and I am poor, you don't treat me as
a human being at all.

You have rice for your geese, ducks, pigs, and dogs; is my
mother nothing to you?

Today the two of us will strike hands on my oath that never in
my life will I come to your gate again.

Guo Ju, afraid of more blows, has to retreat . . .

Uncle (*sings*):

. . . With a blow at every step I force him out of the gate.

Guo Ju has been forced out of the gate; turning my back, I
push the gate closed.

You and I will travel separate roads until we die; I will not open
my gate to you even if you are dying.

Guo (*weeping*): I tell you, Uncle, you savage—this child has not
eaten for three meals and could [not] fend off the blows of your
club. Uncle, you savage!

[Humiliated, Guo exits, meets a friend in the market, borrows
money and buys two buns. He returns home and calls to his wife
from the gate.]

Suzhen [Guo's wife] (*sings*):

Yao Suzhen is in the front room when suddenly she hears someone at the gate.

I get down from the bed but do not leave; holding my baby I say a few things to Mother:

Take good care of yourself here, I am going to the gate to see who it is.

I tell Mother I am going outside, just a little ways to the front gate.

Opening the gate, I see my husband standing there.

Outside the gate is not a place to talk; let us go into our hut and talk.

I lead my husband through the gate, and we soon arrive at the hut.

I give my husband a place to sit.

Guo *(sings):*

I sit down and my tears overflow.

Suzhen *(sings):*

As soon as my husband sits down, I can see from his expression that something is wrong.

His hair is disheveled and his face is pale, but I don't know why.

I sit down facing him and speak respectfully:

You went to Uncle's house to borrow rice—how much did you borrow?

Husband, please give it to me and I'll cook some, to satisfy Mother's hunger.

Guo *(sings):*

If you hadn't brought up borrowing rice it would have been all right, but bringing it up is truly painful. . . . [Guo tells her what happened at his uncle's house and hands her the buns.]

Suzhen *(sings):*

. . . And I take them [the buns] in my hands.

Husband, please wait in the hut; I will go to the sick room to see Mother and try to explain it to her.

Suzhen goes into the sick room and with one word awakens her mother.

Mother *(sings):*

Suddenly I hear my daughter's voice, there's nothing I can do but open my worried eyes.

Ah, it is my son's wife, holding my grandson.

I don't crave either sour or spicy flavors—all I can think of is the aroma of rice gruel.

I would like to have some rice right now—then I'd get better and could leave this bed.

If there is no rice for me, then I am bound to see the King of the Underworld.

I sent my son off to borrow some rice and bring it back here.

I tell my daughter-in-law to cook some rice, to make a bowl of nice rice for Mother to eat.

Suzhen *(sings):*

If you hadn't brought up borrowing rice it would have been all right, but bringing it up is truly painful. . . . [Suzhen recounts Guo's tale.]

Mother *(sings):*

As I take the *shaobing* [buns] I become angry.

I curse you, Brother, you are not human—remember the year when we were rich and you were poor and you borrowed gold and silver from us Guos?

Now when you are rich and we are poor, you don't treat our Guo Ju like a human being.

You said your rice was to feed your chickens, ducks, geese, and dogs; you did not think of what I am to you at all.

If I get better I will stand in front of your gate, you dog.

Then I'll give you what I owe you, and everything you owe me, principal and interest, will be taken back to my house.

She curses the old dog once more, and looks at the *shaobing* to see if they are real.

I will eat one of these *shaobing* and save the other to feed my grandson.

If I starve to death it won't matter much—I'm afraid that my grandson will starve to death.

If my grandson starves to death it will be very serious, for the root of the Guo family will be cut off. . . . [She gives the other bun to Guo for the baby.]

Guo *(sings):*

How painful it is to take this *shaobing*! It's like our little baby is taking food out of Mother's mouth.

Oh, Mother! What feeling is it that makes you still want this little baby?

I say we should just give our little baby to someone else to raise and use the extra food to be filial.

Suzhen *(sings):*

You say we should give our baby to someone else to raise; but if that person should beat or curse him, his mother's heart would break.

I say it would be better to bury him alive, and use the extra
food to be filial.

Guo *(sings):*

What you say, wife, I cannot believe.

Suzhen *(sings):*

I will swear an oath to Heaven.

I come before you and with folded hands fall to my knees.

If I am not telling the truth about wanting to bury our baby,
hereafter I will certainly be struck by the Five Thunders! . . .

[Both exit to get implements for the burial.]

Heavenly Official Who Increases Blessings enters.

Heavenly Official *(speaks):* I am the Heavenly Official Who Increases Blessings. Guo Ju is going to bury his baby for the sake of
his mother. I must go first and bury eighteen pieces of Heavenly
gold and silver. With my treasure-sword I open the earth, open it
three feet deep and bury the gold and silver. The eighteen pieces
of gold and silver I've buried Guo Ju can use to be filial to his
mother. *[Exits.]. . .*

[Guo, his wife and son leave the village. On the trail Suzhen
talks with her husband.]

Suzhen *(sings):*

To some wealth comes, to others poverty.

Guo *(sings):*

Can it be that Uncle has bought ten thousand years of wealth?

Suzhen *(sings):*

Can it be that our poverty is bound to a deep karmic root?

Guo *(sings):*

The Heavenly Official Who Increases Blessings has turned his
back on us;

Suzhen *(sings):*

The hungry ghosts of the starved will not leave our house.

Guo *(sings):*

May the Heavenly Official Who Increases Blessings please
come to our house . . .

Suzhen *(sings):*

. . . And drive away the hungry ghosts of the starved.

Guo *(sings):*

Heavenly Official Who Increases Blessings, we invite you to
our house;

Suzhen *(sings):*

We will give wine and food to your heart's content.

Guo *(sings)*:
　　When you hit a board fence then the high is brought low;
Suzhen *(sings)*:
　　Of ten poor men, nine once were rich.
Guo *(sings)*:
　　Though the leaves of the *wutong* tree may fall, the trunk survives;
Suzhen *(sings)*:
　　Just get rid of the branches and twigs and wait for the spring.
Guo *(sings)*:
　　Even the realm of the Lord of a Myriad Years [the emperor] sometimes collapses and shatters;
Suzhen *(sings)*:
　　The affairs of this world are decided by fate, not by men.
Guo *(sings)*:
　　Though the fierce tiger is skin and bones, his heart is still heroic.
Suzhen *(sings)*:
　　Though a gentleman is poor, he is not poor in will.
Guo *(sings)*:
　　Liu Xiu of the Han dynasty [Emperor Wu] painted tigers and climbed mountains;
Suzhen *(sings)*:
　　Yuan Dan was bitten by a tiger while gathering firewood.
Guo *(sings)*:
　　All I want is that the poor do not have to be fearful. . . .
Guo *(sings)*:
　　Precedence at a banquet is not determined by age;
Suzhen *(sings)*:
　　Those whose clothes are best are treated best.
Guo *(sings)*:
　　Neighbors, if you don't believe me, just you look around;
Suzhen *(sings)*:
　　The first ones to be toasted are the ones with lots of cash. . . .
Guo *(sings)*:
　　Don't go any farther, wife!
Suzhen *(sings)*:
　　Is it here that we will bury him?
Guo *(sings)*:
　　Good wife, please climb the hill and see if there are any travelers.

If there's a person on any of the four high roads, we won't bury him and will go back home.

If there's no one on the four high roads, then we'll bury our baby here.

Suzhen *(sings):*

I hear what my husband says and climb the hill to look carefully around.

Suzhen has reached the hilltop, and looks off to the west, and then to the east.

Can it be that our baby is fated to die? There is not a soul on the four roads.

Suzhen comes down from the hill and tells her husband to hurry and dig a hole.

Guo *(sings):*

I hear what my good wife says, and dig a grave for our baby.

I take a shovelful, and another; I strike once with the mattock, and once again.

While I am finishing the hole, keep the baby occupied as you wait by the road.

Suzhen *(sings):*

I hear what my husband says, and keep the baby occupied as I wait by the road.

I sit on the ground and open my ragged jacket, patches upon patches.

I put the nipple in my boy's mouth, and before long his little belly is as tight as a drum.

Our little baby, not knowing he is to die, gives a tiny smile and tries to stand up in his mother's arms.

As our little baby is on the point of dying in the dirt, I entrust him to you.

I hand over our dear baby to you . . .

Guo *(sings):*

. . . And I take him in my arms.

If our little baby dies in the dirt, he will lodge an accusation against me in the court of the King of the Underworld.

Lord Yama will weigh your accusation, and bring your father to the Dark City.

If you testify against me, I will be pitched with a trident into a vat of boiling oil.

This is the punishment for anyone who buries a little baby alive, blaming us for something we were too poor to avoid.

I hand over the baby to you, so I can dig the hole deeper.

I can't lift another shovelful, [two characters illegible] I fall to the ground.

My vision dims, my head swims—I have not eaten for three
meals, how can I have the strength to dig a hole?
Before long I stop digging, and tell my wife to bury our son.

Suzhen *(sings):*
I crawl forward a few inches on my knees and look into the
hole.
But it is not just a hole in the ground, it is my baby's grave.
If I put my baby in that hole he will scratch at the dirt with his
hands and push at it with his feet.
Your warm, breathing body, that cold dirt—all I can do is hug
my baby tighter.
I think you haven't dug the hole deep enough; the wolves that
seize, the dogs that tear will break my heart.
I ask my husband to dig the hole deeper, to dig it deep enough
to cover our son.

Guo *(sings):*
Guo Ju is angry, his rage pours out; he heaps curses on his
wife's head:
Remember what you said at home? You should not have made
a vow to Heaven.
[Because of your vow] it is impossible to not bury him, and if
we bury him you will escape [divine punishment].
Looking toward my house in the distance I call to my old
mother; Mother who raised me, why don't you reply?
When Mother dies I will put on deep mourning; but who will
have a funeral for me when I die?
I turn my back on my house; gaze at my baby, gaze at the hole.
Little baby, you are a foot and a half long, but the hole is only
a foot.
I dig out another shovelful, and another; hack out another
chunk, and another.
Three shovelfuls, four shovelfuls—and bright silver gleams in
the hole!

Suzhen *(speaks):* Oh, my son, I can't look at you!

Guo *(speaks):* My son! Don't cry! [*Laughs.*]

Suzhen *(speaks):* How can you laugh at such a time?!

Guo *(speaks):* There's silver!

Suzhen *(speaks):* Oh, my God! I've never seen silver!

Guo *(speaks):* Wife, embrace me! Ai-ya! Eighteen pieces of silver and gold! Wife, don't do anything, I'm going to take some
pieces home to be filial to Mother!

(Sings)
High blue Heaven cannot be deceived.

Suzhen *(sings):*
    Don't laugh at poor people wearing rags.
Guo *(sings):*
    Everyone desires riches and children.
Suzhen *(sings):*
    Wealth and glory are bestowed by Heaven.
Guo *(speaks):* Yes, wealth and glory are bestowed by Heaven. Now let us go and be filial to Mother. Husband and wife make obeisance to the sky, ha-ha, oh ha-ha-ha!

An Essay on Landscape Painting

Guo Xi

In traditional Chinese landscape painting, artists sought to portray the spirit of natural beauty in order to enable observers of their paintings to escape from their everyday lives and enter into a peaceful spiritual realm. They believed that this experience molded men and women of good character. Imperial Chinese society placed great store on artistic ability. Emperors were lauded for their artistic talents, and in the entrance examinations civil servants were required to paint or illustrate poems like the following: "When I return from trampling flowers, the hoofs of my horse are fragrant."

In the following extract, eleventh-century painter Guo Xi, known as the greatest landscape painter of his day, describes his views on his art in *An Essay on Landscape Painting*, which influenced the work of Chinese and Japanese landscape painters for the next several centuries. In the essay, Guo Xi says the artist's purpose is to become one with nature in order to convey its true spirit. Guo Xi's son, who collected his father's sayings to create this essay, begins the extract.

When I was a little boy with pigtails, I followed my late father on wanderings among springs and rocks. Each time he put his brush to paper, he used to say: "There is a method in landscape painting. How dare an artist paint in a careless manner?" Whenever I had listened to one of his opinions, I wrote it down immediately in my note-book. Now having collected several hundreds of these, I cannot let them slip into oblivion; therefore I present them to lovers of landscapes. . . .

Kuo Hsi's Comments on Landscapes

Why does a virtuous man take delight in landscapes? It is for these reasons: that in a rustic retreat he may nourish his nature;

Kuo Hsi (Guo Xi), *An Essay on Landscape Painting*. London: John Murray, 1949.

that amid the carefree play of streams and rocks, he may take delight; that he may constantly meet in the country fishermen, woodcutters, and hermits, and see the soaring of the cranes, and hear the crying of the monkeys. The din of the dusty world and the locked-in-ness of human habitations are what human nature habitually abhors; while, on the contrary, haze, mist, and the haunting spirits of the mountains are what human nature seeks, and yet can rarely find. . . .

Having no access to the landscapes, the lover of forest and stream, the friend of mist and haze, enjoys them only in his dreams. How delightful then to have a landscape painted by a skilled hand! Without leaving the room, at once, he finds himself among the streams and ravines; the cries of the birds and monkeys are faintly audible to his senses; light on the hills and reflection on the water, glittering, dazzle his eyes. Does not such a scene satisfy his mind and captivate his heart? That is why the world values the true significance of the painting of mountains. If this is not recognized, and the landscapes are roughly and carelessly approached, then is it not like spoiling a magnificent view and polluting the pure wind? . . .

It is the considered judgment of mankind that there are landscapes in which one can travel, landscapes which can be gazed upon, landscapes in which one may ramble, and landscapes in which one may dwell. When any painting reaches one of these standards, it enters the category of the pre-excellent. However, one suitable for travelling in or gazing upon is not as successful as one in which one may dwell or ramble. Why is this? Look at the landscape paintings of to-day. They portray mountains and streams spread over the earth for several hundred miles. These are all accepted as suitable for living in or rambling in; yet only three- to four-tenths of the whole are deservedly so. Nevertheless these few beautiful landscapes arouse in the superior man a yearning for forest and stream. Therefore, the painters should work with this idea in mind, and the beholders should study the paintings with this same idea. This is what is meant by not losing sight of the fundamental idea. . . .

In painting a scene, irrespective of its size or scope, an artist should concentrate his spirit upon the essential nature of his work. If he fails to get at the essential, he will fail to present the soul of his theme. Discipline should give his picture dignity. Without dignity depth is impossible. Diligence and reverence will make his work complete. Without that diligence it will remain incomplete.

Therefore when the artist is lazily forcing himself to work and is failing to draw from the very depths of his resources, then his painting is weak and soft and lacking in decisiveness. His fault is that of not concentrating on the essential. If he is confused and has cloudy ideas, then the forms become obscure and uncertain. His fault is that of not putting his whole soul into his work. If he approaches his painting too lightly, then the forms are likely to be disjointed and inharmonious. His fault is lack of dignity. If he neglects his work out of conceit, then the composition is careless and incomplete. His fault is lack of diligence. Therefore indecisiveness leads to faulty analysis, dullness to a lack of elegance, disjointedness to a want of proportion, incompleteness to a lack of orderly arrangement. These are the chief faults of the artist. These matters, however, can only be discussed with enlightened beings. . . .

To learn to draw a flower, it is best to place a blossoming plant in a deep hollow in the ground and look down upon it. Then all its qualities may be grasped. To learn to draw bamboo, take a branch and cast its shadow on a while wall on a moonlight night; then its true outline can be obtained. To learn to paint landscape, too, the method is the same. An artist should identify himself with the landscape and watch it until its significance is revealed to him. The rivers and valleys of a fine landscape, viewed at a distance, show their contours; viewed at close range, they show their component parts. . . .

Majesty of Nature

A great mountain is so stately that it becomes the master of multitudinous others arranged about it in order. It becomes the great master of the hills and slopes, forests and valleys, far and near, small and large. Its appearance is that of an emperor sitting majestically in all his glory, accepting the service of and giving audience to his subjects, without sign of arrogance or haughtiness.

A tall pine tree is so stately that it becomes a leader amongst the other trees. It stretches out accordingly over vines and creepers, grass and trees, a leader for those who are unable to support themselves. Its state is like that of a prince who wins the approval of his age and receives the services of lesser people, without sign of anxiety or vexation. . . .

Spring and summer views of the mountains have certain aspects; autumn and winter views have others. . . . The spring mountain is wrapped in an unbroken stretch of dreamy haze and mist, and men are joyful; the summer mountain is rich with shady foliage, and men are peaceful; the autumn mountain is serene and calm, with leaves falling, and men are solemn; the winter mountain is heavy with storm clouds and withdrawn, and men are forlorn.

The sight of such pictured mountains arouses in man exactly corresponding moods. It is as if he were actually in those mountains. They exist as if they were real and not painted. The blue haze and white path arouse a longing to walk there; the sunset on a quiet stream arouses a longing to gaze upon it; the sight of hermits and ascetics arouses a longing to dwell with them; rocks and streams arouse a longing to saunter among them. The contemplation of good paintings nourishes this longing. The places become real, and the meaning of these pictures is wonderful. . . .

The Meaning of Painting

Although people know that I paint with a brush, little do they realize how difficult it is to paint. In the *Chuang-tzŭ* [a written work of the Taoist philosopher Chuang-Tzu (399–295 B.C.)] it is said that a painter at work "took off his clothes and squatted down cross-legged." That is indeed the true way of the artist. He should nourish in his bosom cheerfulness and a happy mood. That is, if he can develop a natural, sincere, gentle, and honest heart, then he will immediately be able to comprehend the aspects of tears and smiles and of objects, pointed or oblique, bent or inclined, and they will be so clear in his mind that he will be able to put them down spontaneously with his paint brush.

It is said that Ku K'ai-chih [famous landscape painter] of the Tsin dynasty [265–589] always built a high pavilion as his place of painting. He was truly a man of wide vision in the ancient time. For, without such aids, an artist's thoughts become depressed, melancholy, or clogged, and he broods over some trivial matter. Then how can he paint the real forms of objects or express emotions? For example, an artisan wishing to make a harp finds a solitary dryandra [tree] from Mount I-yang [near the Tsin dynasty's capital]. Having skill and knowing the mysteries of his art, although the tree is still rooted in the ground and the leaves and branches still uncut he immediately has a clear mental picture of a finished lute. A master like Lei [early imperial Chinese master painter] has that kind of eye for his material. But with troubled thoughts and a worn-out body a dull and insensitive man would see the pointed chisels and sharp knives before him and not know where to begin. Then how could he be expected to make "a lute of half-burnt wood" which would have five mystic notes or would sound forth most delightfully with the clear wind and the flowing stream?

Painting from Poetry

It has been said by the ancients that poetry is a picture without form, and painting is a poem with form. Philosophers often discoursed on this topic and it has been my guiding principle. In my leisure hours, therefore, I often perused the poetry of the Tsin and T'ang [618–906] dynasties as well as the modern, and found that some of the beautiful lines give full expression to the inmost thoughts of men's souls, and describe vividly the scenery before men's eyes. Nevertheless, unless I dwell in peace and sit in leisure, with windows cleaned, the desk dusted, incense burning, and ten thousand worries drowned and subdued, I am not able to get at the mood and meaning of beautiful lines, think excellent thoughts, and imagine the subtle feelings described in them. The same thing is true of painting. It is not easy to grasp its meaning. When I am responsive and at one with my surroundings and have achieved perfect coordination of mind and hand, then I start to paint freely and expertly, as the proper standard of art demands. Men of to-day, however, are swept away by their impulses and feelings, and rush to complete their work.

Therefore, I, Ssŭ, have set down the following poems, some of which my father was fond of reciting. He considered that some of them contained themes appropriate for painting. To them I have added others which I have sought out for myself. I list them below.

Gazing at Mount Nu I
On the peak of Mount Nu I the spring snow is gone.

By the roadside apricot flowers begin to bud.
Not knowing when I can fulfil my heart's desire to depart,
In despair I turn back my carriage at the rustic bridge.

By Yang Shih-e.

A Visit to a Mountain Retreat

Alone I set out to visit a mountain retreat, now stopping, now
    proceeding again.
Thatched cottages are linked behind the pine branches.
Though the host hears my voice, the gate is not yet open;
By the fence over the wild lettuce flutters a yellow butterfly.

By Ch'ang-sun Tso-fu. . . .

The bamboo thicket sieves the rain drops;
The high peak holds the evening glow.

By Hsia-hou Shu-chien. . . .

Clouds wait brooding for snow and hang heavily over the earth;
The wail of autumn is uninterrupted as the wild geese sweep
    over the sky.

By Ch'ien Wei-yen. . . .

Together we gazed on distant waters;
Alone I sit in a lone boat.

By Chang Ku.

Chronology

ca. 2852–2595 B.C.
Three legendary founders—Fu Xi, Shennong, and Huangdi (the Yellow Emperor)—rule China.

ca. 2205–1766 B.C.
The Xia dynasty rules China.

ca. 1700–1027 B.C.
The Shang dynasty rules China and begins the classical period of Chinese history.

ca. 1100–770 B.C.
The Western Chou dynasty rules China as a feudal state.

770–249 B.C.
The Eastern Chou dynasty rules China encompassing the Spring and Autumn periods and the period of the Warring States.

604–531 B.C.
The legendary founder of Taoism, the mythical Lao-tzu, is born and dies.

551–479 B.C.
Confucius is born and dies.

215–214 B.C.
The Great Wall is unified.

2211–206 B.C.
The Qin dynasty unifies China for the first time.

206 B.C.–A.D. 220
The imperial period of China's history begins with the rule of the Han dynasty. Confucianism is adopted as the state ideology.

64

Early signs of the introduction of Buddhism appear with the founding of the White Horse Monastery in Luoyang.

220–589

National unity disintegrates with the fall of the Han dynasty. The Period of Division follows.

589–618

The Sui dynasty reunites northern and southern China under one rule.

618–907

The Tang dynasty rules as a wealthy and powerful empire. Xi'an, the capital city, is the largest city in the world.

907–960

A period of division with five dynasties in the north and ten kingdoms in the south follows the decline of the Tang dynasty. Foot binding of Chinese upper-class women is introduced.

960–1127

The Northern Song dynasty rules China and establishes its capital at Kaifeng.

1127–1279

The Southern Song dynasty rules China with its capital at Hangzhou, the largest and most culturally and technologically advanced city in the world.

1279–1294

The Mongols take over China and establish the Yuan dynasty with Kublai Khan as emperor.

1275–1292

Marco Polo serves Kublai Khan.

1368–1644

The Ming dynasty re-establishes Han dynasty rule.

1421
Beijing is made the capital of China.

1472–1529
Wang Yangming, a major philosopher of neo-Confucianism, lives.

1644–1912
The Qing dynasty is established by Manchurians.

1839–1842
China is defeated in the first Opium War with Great Britain and cedes Hong Kong to the British.

1850–1864
The Taiping Rebellion leads to civil war, which weakens the Qing dynasty, making it vulnerable to foreign imperialism.

1856–1858
The second Opium War ends with the Treaties of Tianjin in which China makes more concessions to Europe.

1884–1885
France defeats China and establishes French Indochina (Vietnam).

1894–1895
During the Sino-Japanese War, China loses domination of Korea to Japan.

1898
During the Hundred Days Reform, the Qing emperor tries to transform China into a constitutional monarchy but is thwarted by the conservative Empress Dowager Cixi.

1900
During the Boxer Rebellion, the people revolt in an effort to expel foreigners from China.

1908

The last Qing emperor, Pu Yi, ascends the throne.

1911

Sun Yat-sen leads the revolution against the Qing dynasty.

1912

The Qing emperor abdicates and the Republic of China is established, ending more than two millennia of Chinese imperial rule.

1949

After a prolonged period of rivalry between the Nationalists and the Communists, Mao Zedong, the Communist Party leader, establishes the People's Republic of China.

1978

After Mao Zedong's death in 1976, Deng Xiaoping liberalizes the economy and opens China up to the world.

1989

Students demonstrate in favor of political reform in Beijing's Tiananmen Square. The People's Liberation Army violently suppresses the demonstration and many people are killed.

1997

Deng Xiaoping dies. Hong Kong returns to Chinese control after 150 years of British rule.

For Further Research

Books

Charles Benn, *Daily Life in Traditional China: The Tang Dynasty.* Westport, CT: Greenwood, 2002.

James Cahill, *The Painter's Practice: How Artists Lived and Worked in Traditional China.* New York: Columbia University Press, 1994.

Victoria Cass, *Dangerous Women: Warriors, Grannies, and Geishas of the Ming.* New York: Rowman & Littlefield, 1999.

K.C. Chang, ed., *Food in Chinese Culture: Anthropological and Historical Perspectives.* New Haven, CT: Yale University Press, 1977.

William Theodore de Bary and Irene Bloom, eds., *Sources of Chinese Tradition.* Vol. 1. New York: Columbia University Press, 1999.

William Theodore de Bary and Richard Lufrano, eds., *Sources of Chinese Tradition.* Vol. 2. New York: Columbia University Press, 1999.

Patricia Buckley Ebrey, ed., *Chinese Civilization and Society. A Sourcebook.* New York: Free Press, 1981.

———, *Confucianism and Family Rituals in Imperial China.* Princeton, NJ: Princeton University Press, 1991.

———, *Women and the Family in Chinese History.* New York: Routledge, 2003.

Fu Qifeng, *Chinese Acrobatics Through the Ages.* Beijing: Foreign Languages Press, 1985.

Fu Shen, *Chapters from a Floating Life: Autobiography of a Chinese Artist.* London: Oxford University Press, 1960.

Jacques Gernet, *Daily Life in China on the Eve of the Mongol Invasion, 1250–1276.* Stanford, CA: Stanford University Press, 1962.

———, *A History of Chinese Civilization.* Cambridge, UK: Cambridge University Press, 1996.

Valerie Hanson, *Negotiating Daily Life in Traditional China.* New Haven, CT: Yale University Press, 1995.

Linda Cooke Johnson, *Cities of Jiangnan in Late Imperial China.* Albany: State University of New York, 1993.

Anne Kinney, ed., *Chinese Views of Childhood*. Honolulu: University of Hawaii Press, 1995.

Dorothy Ko, *Teachers of the Inner Chambers: Women and Culture in Seventeenth Century China*. Stanford, CA: Stanford University Press, 1994.

Norman Kutcher, *Mourning in Late Imperial China: Filial Piety and the State*. Cambridge, UK: Cambridge University Press, 1999.

Howard S. Levy, *Chinese Footbinding. The History of a Curious Erotic Custom*. New York: Bell, 1967.

Michael Loewe, *Everyday Life in Imperial China During the Han Period, 202 B.C.–A.D. 220*. London: Carousel Books, 1973.

Donald S. Lopez Jr., *Religions of China in Practice*. Princeton, NJ: Princeton University Press, 1996.

Joseph Needham, "Medicine and Chinese Culture." In *Clerks and Craftsmen in China and the West*. Cambridge, UK: Cambridge University Press, 1970.

———, *Science and Civilization in China*. 21 vols. Cambridge, UK: Cambridge University Press, 1962–1998.

Maoshing Ni, trans., *The Yellow Emperor's Classic of Medicine*. Boston: Shambala, 1995.

William Nienhauser, ed., *The Indiana Companion to Traditional Chinese Literature*. Bloomington: Indiana University Press, 1998.

Deborah Sommer, ed., *Chinese Religion: An Anthology of Sources*. New York: Oxford University Press, 1995.

Matthew H. Sommer, *Sex, Law, and Society in Late Imperial China*. Stanford, CA: Stanford University Press, 2000.

Nancy Steinhardt, ed., *Chinese Traditional Architecture*. New York: China Institute in America, 1984.

Arthur Waley, *An Introduction to the Study of Chinese Painting*. New York: Grove, 1958.

———, *The Poetry and Career of Li Po*. New York: Macmillan, 1958.

Periodicals

William Dolby, "The Origins of Chinese Puppetry," *Bulletin of the School of Oriental and African Studies*, vol. 1, 1978.

Laurence Picken, "Tang Music and Musical Instruments," *T'oung Pao*, vol. 55, 1969.

J.K. Rideout, "The Rise of the Eunuchs During the Tang Dynasty," *Asia Major*, vols. 1 and 3, 1949, 1953.

Nathan Sivin, "State, Cosmos, and Body in the Last Three Centuries B.C.," *Harvard Journal of Asiatic Studies*, vol. 55, no. 1, June 1995.

Web Sites

The Analects by Confucius, http://classics.mit.edu/Confucius/analects.html. The Massachusetts Institute of Technology Web site gives a translation of the analects of Confucius with commentary and includes biographical data on the Chinese sage.

CHINA—a Country Study, http://memory.loc.gov/frd/cs/cntoc.html. This site gives the table of contents for the full text of *China: A Country Study.* Researched and edited by Library of Congress staff, the work includes a history of imperial China and information on traditional cultural, religious, and social life of the Chinese people.

Chinaknowledge, www.chinaknowledge.de/guide.html. Compiled by Chinese scholars, this site provides information on China's geography, history, philosophy, religion, literature, and the arts in the imperial era and beyond.

China the Beautiful, www.chinapage.com/main2.html. This site focuses on the arts—literature, painting, poetry, opera, Chinese festivals, and more for the imperial era and contemporary China.

Index